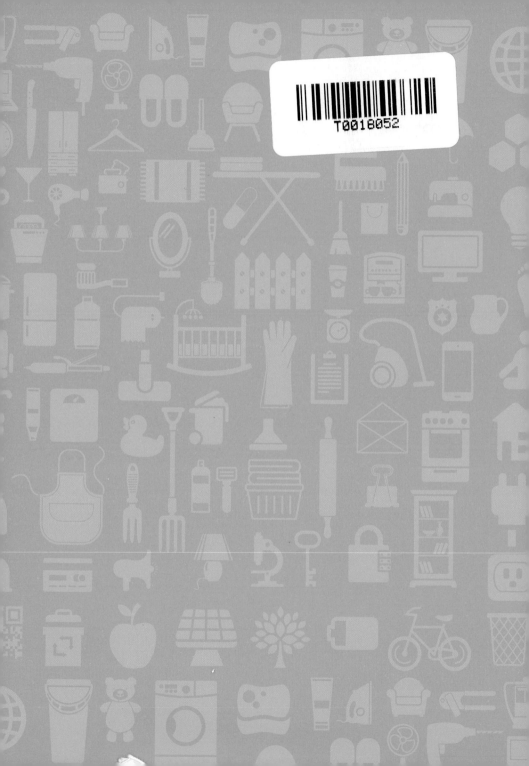

ADULTING 101

Life Skills All Teens Should Know

PETER PAUPER PRESS, INC.

RYE BROOK, NEW YORK

PETER PAUPER PRESS
Fine Books and Gifts Since 1928

OUR COMPANY

In 1928, at the age of twenty-two, Peter Beilenson began printing books on a small press in the basement of his parents' home in Larchmont, New York. Peter—and later, his wife, Edna—sought to create fine books that sold at "prices even a pauper could afford."

Today, still family owned and operated, Peter Pauper Press continues to honor our founders' legacy—and our customers' expectations—of beauty, quality, and value.

Written by Hannah Beilenson

Designed by Heather Zschock

Images used under license from Shutterstock.com

Copyright © 2023 Peter Pauper Press, Inc.
Manufactured for Peter Pauper Press, Inc.
3 International Drive
Rye Brook, NY 10573 USA

Published in the United Kingdom and Europe by
Peter Pauper Press, Inc. c/o White Pebble International
Units 2-3, Spring Business Park
Stanbridge Road
Havant, Hampshire PO9 2GJ, UK

Library of Congress Cataloging-in-Publication Data

Names: Beilenson, Hannah, author.
Title: Adulting 101 : life skills all teens should know /
written by Hannah Beilenson.
Description: Hampshire, UK : Peter Pauper Press, Inc., [2023] | Audience:
Grades 10-12 | Summary: "A teenager's guide to all the skills you never
learned in school. From low-stress laundry and kitchen hacks, to
navigating health insurance and healthy friendships, this book is full
of tips to help you face a crazy world head-on"—Provided by publisher.

Identifiers: LCCN 2022050390 | ISBN 9781441340566 (hardcover)
Subjects: LCSH: Teenagers--Life skills guides. | Life skills.
Classification: LCC HQ796 .B3447 2023 | DDC 646.700835—dc23/eng/20221027
LC record available at https://lccn.loc.gov/2022050390

Visit us at www.peterpauper.com

CONTENTS

Growing up is never easy.
We think it happens when you reach
a certain age, accomplish a goal,
acquire a house, or reach a milestone,
but it doesn't stop.
-Ranjani Rao

LET'S DO THIS

First things first. No one expects you to just read this book and suddenly be an adult. The truth is, most adults only feel like adults, like, a quarter of the time. Growing up (whatever that means) is a lifelong process—there's no test you pass, no moment when you're old enough that it all magically makes sense. You just live in this world for a while and start to get the hang of what you need to. That said, getting older comes with its own set of challenges (and privileges). This book is full of skills you'll need to face those challenges head-on. You'll probably find that you already know a few skills in this book and haven't considered others. Even if you don't need some of these skills right now, keep them in the back of your mind, and know that you'll have this book handy when the time comes to put them to use.

Adulting isn't always fun, but it can pave the way for enjoyment. No one is out there budgeting because they get a kick out of it. They budget so they can buy a new gaming console, travel to cool places, or order more takeout. And skills that just plain suck are sometimes necessary anyway. You don't unclog a toilet because that activity secretly rules. You do it because you need a usable toilet. (Sorry in advance to the toilet-cleaning fandom.)

You may also come across skills that you can't commit to doing. Or you may find that you need to hack the way you approach a given skill. Not only is that okay, it's totally normal. One of the biggest parts of adulting is creating a life tailored to your own needs. You are not alone in this world, and no single person can or should do everything. It's okay if you can't or won't cook meat, if creating a morning routine isn't feasible, or if cleaning your room isn't a one-person job.

So what's the reason for any of this? There's not just one. It's nice to strengthen relationships, to gain independence, to finish a project, to know yourself. This book is here to help you start making those things happen.

TAKING CARE OF YOU

Love or hate it, you've gotta live in it—and life is better when you treat your body as a friend. With these tips, personal care doesn't have to be a slog.

SLEEP EASY

Lots of people have trouble falling asleep. Try these quick tips to help your mind and body drift off. Mix and match to find what works for you!

Soothing Sips

Before bed, drink a cup of something warm to calm your system and prepare for sleep. Warm milk or chamomile tea may help on restless nights. Milk contains tryptophan (which can release mood-boosting, relaxing serotonin in your brain) and melatonin (a hormone that helps regulate your sleep rhythms). Chamomile has been used since forever (well, for at least five thousand years) to induce sleepiness, soothe upset stomachs, and calm anxiety. Just make sure that whatever you drink is caffeine-free and not too sugary.

White Noise

True "white noise" creates a balanced blend of all sound frequencies, resulting in a sort of soothing static. White noise or any similar repetitive sounds may help you sleep. You don't need a special machine—you can use a fan, or find apps with calming sounds like ocean waves, light rain, and indistinct chatter on your phone. You can also listen to soothing podcasts at a low volume. Just make sure to choose a topic that won't make you want to stay up and listen.

Breathe Deep

You know the old saying about counting sheep to fall asleep? The rhythmic activity of counting can help you relax. Similarly, practicing deep breathing can release tension from your body. In bed, try belly breathing. Place one hand on your upper chest, and the other below your rib cage. Slowly breathe in through your nose, drawing the breath down to your stomach. Feel how your back and rib cage expand. Then, slowly exhale through your mouth, letting the air leave your stomach without collapsing that space in your rib cage. The hand on your chest should remain still, while the hand on your belly rises and falls. Continue until you feel chilled out.

Relax Your Muscles and Your Mind

Starting with your toes, gradually tense and relax your muscle groups one at a time. As you relax each group, moving from your feet to your calves, and upward toward your neck and head, visualize the tension leaving your body. This goes for any anxious thoughts that settle in at night, too. Just picture yourself releasing them, one by one, and let them drift away from you.

Sleep Supplements

Your body naturally produces melatonin (a hormone that helps control

the sleep-wake cycle), and it's one of the most common supplements for insomnia. Varying doses are available, but as little as 0.3 mg can improve sleep quality. Just check with a doctor before you start supplements, especially if you have medical conditions.

WAKE-UP TIPS

You're probably familiar with waking up earlier than you'd prefer, and odds are you'll have to keep doing it. But if you can get up without feeling too groggy, you can lower the chance of being in a terrible mood all day. Try some of these tricks to make getting out of bed a little easier.

Keep the Time Consistent

If you have to get up at six a.m. on weekdays, it's tempting to sleep past noon on Saturdays. But "catching up" on sleep doesn't really work. Instead, you're confusing your circadian rhythm (your body's natural alarm clock). You'll have an easier time waking up if your alarm is set for a similar time each morning.

Make Use of Light

Screens, fluorescent lights, alarm clocks, and busy schedules all confuse your body about when it's time to sleep. Natural light can help you reset in the morning. Keep your shades open and let the rising sun help pull you out of bed. If you don't have windows in your room or have to wake up before the sun rises, you can also use a lamp that imitates sunlight.

Pre-Bedtime Prep

Shave a few minutes off your morning routine by getting things ready when your brain's still working. Putting some clothes for tomorrow in arm's reach before bed can spare you the half-asleep fumble when you wake up.

Keep Your Alarm Out of Reach

If you press snooze fifteen times before you can actually open your eyes, try leaving your phone or alarm clock on the opposite side of the room. Instead of pressing snooze and falling back asleep, you'll have to get up and out of bed to silence the alarm.

Plan a Morning Treat

Getting out of bed will obviously suck if it's only because school and work are forcing you. Try giving yourself something to look forward to each morning—delicious food, a cup of tea, an exciting outfit, or a private ritual, like journaling or a warm shower. Taking a few minutes to treat your mind and body can make a big difference. If you don't have time for breakfast, a quick bite is better than nothing. Even a little self-care goes a long way.

Avoid Your Phone

Checking social media before even brushing your teeth is like pouring poison on your brain. Leave your phone out of sight until your feet are firmly on the ground, and you may find that with nothing to distract you, you'll dodge the morning stress a little longer.

EAT TO ENERGIZE

We'll talk more about food in the next chapter, but let's start with tips for energy-friendly eating. Whether you're going for a hike or just trying to maintain your mental energy until lunch, it's good to fuel up on foods that are filling, sustaining, and tasty.

The building blocks of filling meals and snacks are **carbohydrates**, **proteins**, and **fats**. Carbs give you instant energy, protein helps build muscle and supports bodily function, and fats allow your body to store energy and make hormones. When these three macronutrients are combined, you'll feel satisfied and have energy to power through the day.

Try combining some of the foods from these lists to energize your body!

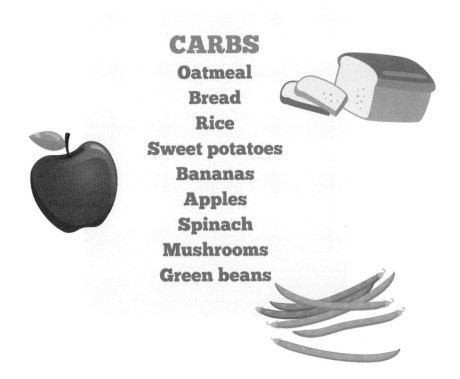

CARBS
Oatmeal
Bread
Rice
Sweet potatoes
Bananas
Apples
Spinach
Mushrooms
Green beans

FATS
Avocado
Coconut
Nut butter
Chocolate
Olive oil
Flaxseed
Butter
Cheese

PROTEINS
Eggs
Chicken
Salmon
Turkey
Milk
Tofu
Seeds

ALL IN ONE
Full-fat yogurt
Nuts
Legumes

SIMPLE SKIN CARE

Skin care can seem daunting, but it's more than worth showing this part of your body some love. Use these tips to set up and follow a simple routine, and your skin will soon be feeling better than ever!

How to Wash Your Face

1. Use a gentle, alcohol-free cleanser.

2. Wash with lukewarm water and use your fingertips to apply the cleanser. Other materials can irritate your skin.

3. Rinse and pat dry.

4. Apply moisturizer gently—don't pull too hard on your skin, especially around your eyes.

5. Wash once in the morning and once at night.

Tips for Zits

- You can treat mild pimples yourself with benzoyl peroxide and salicylic acid.

- For blackheads and whiteheads, you can use a retinoid and salicylic acid to help unclog pores.

- For more serious acne, like cysts and nodules, you can meet with a dermatologist to get a higher strength prescription medication.

No matter what, don't pop your pimples! Seriously!
Yes, zits aren't pretty, but a bloody face sure doesn't look any better. Plus, popping pimples can leave permanent scars.

What to Do with Dry Skin

- Use a gentle moisturizer several times a day, within five minutes of bathing, after washing your hands, or whenever your skin feels dry.

- Use a humidifier to add moisture to your skin.

- Avoid using hot water when you shower, as it strips your skin of moisture.

- Guard your skin against UV rays by wearing clothing that protects your skin and sunscreen (at least SPF 30).

When You See Red...

- **Focus on the cause.** Different skin conditions can cause redness, and each condition requires a different course of treatment. Meet with a dermatologist to get a better sense of what's happening to your skin.

- **Check your products.** Certain skin care products, body lotions, and shampoos can irritate your skin. Scan the ingredients for common irritants, and see if removing them from your routine leads to any improvement.

- **Treat your skin gently.** Don't over-exfoliate or scrub too harshly.

HOW TO SHAVE

If you're looking for some quick shaving tips, look no further! If you've come to this page by mistake and are looking for quick *saving* tips, check out page 110.

Shaving Your Face

1. **Wash your face with warm water and a gentle cleanser.** Shaving a clean face reduces irritation and can help prevent ingrown hairs.

2. **Apply shaving cream.** It helps you prevent irritation and get a closer shave.

3. **Use short, light strokes with a razor.** Don't shave from ear to chin.

4. **Shave in the direction of your hair.** Going against the grain puts you at risk of cuts and ingrown hairs.

5. **Rinse and pat dry!** If you've cut yourself, use an alum block to soothe your skin, prevent the spread of bacteria, and reduce bleeding. You look great!

Can I use an electric razor?

Definitely! Electric razors save time, protect sensitive skin, and offer more precise control. Just make sure you buy a model you're comfortable with and read the instructions carefully!

Shaving Your Body

1. **Start in the shower or bathtub.** The warm water will hydrate your skin, making it easier to shave without cutting yourself.

2. **Apply shaving cream.** Just like with your face, shaving cream will help you prevent irritation and get a closer shave.

3. **Think about the grain.** Many will shave their legs going upward against the grain for a closer shave. However, when in doubt, shave with the grain to avoid irritation, especially at the armpits.

4. **Go slowly and gently,** especially around the knees and ankles. Because of their shapes, it's very easy to accidentally cut yourself in these areas.

5. **Rinse and moisturize when finished.** So smooth!

Does shaving make the hair grow back thicker?

Nope! That's a myth. The sharp edge of a razor leaves stubble that you can feel on your skin, which is why some people believe that the hair is growing back thicker.

Do I have to shave?

Definitely not! People shave for lots of reasons, some aesthetic and some practical. But whatever the reason, it's ultimately a personal choice. If you don't feel like shaving, there's no reason to! Human beings have hair all over their bodies and have been ignoring it, changing it, and reveling in it for all of history. Do what you like!

CLEANING YOUR BODY

If only it were as simple as getting into the shower and getting out. Luckily, it's almost that simple! For maximum cleanliness, keep these tips in mind.

Use Warm Water

Water that's too hot can strip your skin of protective oils, like sebum. Sebum seals in moisture, preventing your skin from drying out. It also has antibacterial and antifungal properties to defend against infection.

Soap Up (But Not Everywhere)

Soap is great, but you really only need it on select areas of the body. When you shower, focus on areas prone to odor, like your armpits, buttocks, and feet.

Be Gentle

If you use a body scrub, loofah, or washcloth to remove dead skin, make sure you don't scrub too hard. Over-exfoliating can irritate and dry out your skin, leading to redness, sensitivity, and breakouts. You really shouldn't need to exfoliate more than once or twice a week.

Keep It Clean

Clean and replace loofahs and washcloths regularly. Damp sponges are perfect breeding grounds for bacteria and mildew. If you use them without sanitizing them, you can bring these microscopic fiends in contact with your skin.

Do I have to shower every day?

No! Well, maybe! Everybody is different. For many, showering every other day or even every third day is enough, especially if you're washing your face regularly. However, athletes, those who work outdoors, and those who work with animals may want to shower every day to keep clean.

MOVING YOUR BODY

Yeah, our ancestors ran from wolves and chased gazelles so that we could watch TV and complain about having to go to the grocery store. But the biological perks of staying active still work on our modern bodies. It won't fix all your problems, but exercise can increase alertness, reduce stress, tone muscles, and help with sleep. If you're looking to increase your stamina and strength, these pages have tips to get you started.

Take a Walk

Get those steps in! Walking is not only an excellent foundation for running, it's great exercise on its own. Walking for just half an hour per day can increase heart health, strengthen bones, and boost muscle power.

Run Smart, Not Hard

If you want to be a runner, don't rush, or you'll find yourself exhausted and out of breath fast. Instead, alternate between jogging and walking at different intervals. Walking gives your body time to recover from the stresses of running, and lets you catch your breath. If you want to move for twenty minutes, start by jogging for one minute, walking for four, and repeating until the clock runs out. As you continue running, you'll be able to shift this ratio and jog for longer periods of time.

Warm Up and Cool Down

To reduce soreness and avoid hurting yourself, **warm up** your body for a few minutes before strenuous exercise, and **cool down** afterward. Any light exercise, like walking for five to ten minutes, is great for both warming up and cooling down. Warming up gets your blood flowing to your muscles, so they're ready to handle your workout. Cooling down afterward slowly brings your heartbeat back down to its normal rate, so you don't get dizzy. Stretching the major muscles of areas like your legs, arms, and back can also be helpful.

Make a Routine

It can be difficult to motivate yourself to keep active at first. However, if you make exercise a part of your regular routine, it'll be easier to keep going. Try devoting a specific time each day to your workout, and include incentives to make it more fun. Create a playlist that will get your blood pumping. If you use a treadmill or elliptical machine, watch TV on your phone and time will fly by. Walk, run, or bike to places you enjoy.

Fuel Up

Exercise takes energy, and energy means food. Fuel up with a light, high-carb snack 30 to 60 minutes before your workout to make sure your body is ready to go. If you're going on a long run, eat a high-carb, moderate-protein snack three to four hours before you get started.

Also, make sure to stay hydrated! Water isn't overrated. In most cases, it's the best drink to keep you going during exercise. Sports drinks are recommended mainly for longer workouts in high heat, when you're sweating out a lot of your electrolytes (essential minerals). For shorter or less frequent workouts, the high sugar load outweighs the other benefits.

Rest Your Body

It's important to take time to rest your body and let your muscles recover. If a particular muscle group is sore, give it a day off to repair itself.

> Lots of people work out so they can expand their limits, but there's always such a thing as too much. Don't push to the point of hurting yourself, and don't let other people's standards keep you from listening to what your body needs.

Adapt Your Exercise to Your Body

Not every type of exercise works for every body. If "standard" exercise types aren't right for you, look online for routines and (often free) video classes that suit your needs better. There are chair-based workouts, arm exercises that go easy on your wrists, core workouts that minimize back strain, and much more. Some gyms and studios also host in-person adaptive classes.

HOW TO DO PUSH-UPS AND CRUNCHES (WITHOUT TOTALLY HATING IT)

Push-ups are a great exercise to strengthen your chest, arm muscles, and core, and they suck a lot less when you don't have a PE teacher standing over you. They can be scaled up and down for difficulty, and you don't need any special equipment. Follow the steps below to practice push-ups and crunches safely (and impressively).

Doing a Push-Up

1. Lie face-down on the ground, keeping your feet together.

2. Put your hands on the ground, about shoulder-width apart, with your elbows facing your toes.

3. Curl your toes upward so that the balls of your feet are touching the floor.

4. Raise your body using your arms, keeping your body straight and even.

5. Keeping your body straight, lower yourself with your hands.

6. Repeat until you've completed your set. A good starting set is about ten push-ups, but you can change this number depending on your comfort level.

You can lower the intensity by putting weight on your knees instead of the balls of your feet, or by doing push-ups on a slight incline. You can also step it up a notch by trying one-handed push-ups, or by clapping in mid-air before you lower yourself back down.

Crunch Time

Another no-equipment exercise that you can do at home whenever. Crunches use your own body weight to tone your abs and strengthen your core. Just follow these steps for a satisfying set.

1. Lie down on an exercise mat, thick towel, or carpeted floor.

2. Bend your knees so your feet are flat on the floor, about hip-width apart.

3. Cross your arms across your chest or place your fingertips behind your head. (Just make sure you're not tugging your head up when you do the crunch.)

4. Exhale and raise your shoulder blades off the floor with a smooth, controlled motion. Hold the position for one or two seconds.

5. Gently inhale as you lower your shoulders back down with a slow, steady motion—don't just drop to the floor.

6. Repeat in a set of about twelve crunches.

Note: If you're too tired to do an exercise with correct form—if your back sinks into an arch during pushups, or you're pulling on your neck with each crunch—it's time to rest. Doing exercises incorrectly can hurt you.

FIRST AID BASICS

Accidents happen! For serious injuries, it's important to seek medical advice and treatment. But for everyday cuts, scrapes, twists, and sprains, here are some simple steps to care for your body and support it as it heals.

Cuts and Scrapes

1. Wash your hands thoroughly to avoid infection.

2. Stop the bleeding. While many cuts and scrapes stop bleeding on their own, you may need to apply gentle pressure with a clean cloth or bandage.

3. Clean the cut by rinsing it with water. Wash around the wound with soap, but don't get soap in the wound. Remove any dirt/debris with clean tweezers.

4. Apply an antibiotic or petroleum jelly. This helps keep the surface moist, prevent scarring, and protect against infection.

5. Cover the cut with a bandage or rolled gauze. Change this dressing once a day.

6. Watch for signs of infection and see a doctor if you notice redness, increasing pain, or swelling.

When should I see a doctor?

Whether or not you seek medical care depends on an injury's shape, severity, location, and risk of infection. See a doctor immediately if any of the following is true:

- The shape of the wound is jagged.
- The injury is on your face.
- Edges of the wound are gaping open.
- The bleeding won't stop after ten minutes of pressure.
- It's been five or more years since you last had a tetanus shot.

Twists and Sprains

For minor twists and sprains, you can follow the acronym R.I.C.E. to care for your injury.

- **R** – Rest your injured limb. You don't need to avoid all activity, but try to not put weight on the injured area.

- **I** – Ice the injury. You can use an ice pack, a slush bath, or a compression sleeve filled with cold water to prevent further swelling. Ice as soon as you can for 15- to 20-minute intervals 4 to 8 times a day. Do this for the first two days or until the swelling starts to subside.

- **C** – Compress the injury with a bandage or elastic wrap to promote recovery.

- **E** – Elevate the injury above your heart as often as you can. This helps limit swelling.

As you recover, you can use over-the-counter pain medication, like ibuprofen (common brand names: Advil and Aleve) and acetaminophen (common brand name: Tylenol).

How do I know if it's serious?

Typically, you can tell the severity of a sprain by how bad the pain and swelling are. If you can't bear any weight on the limb, if the joint feels unstable, or if you can't use the joint, seek emergency medical care. If you develop redness that spreads out from the injury, you may have an infection and should see a doctor as soon as possible. If you've injured a body part that has been injured previously, it's also important to see a professional.

CARING FOR COLDS

They're not called "common" for nothing! Most of the time, you don't need to see a doctor for a common cold, but that doesn't mean they're a walk in the park. As you wait for your cold to improve (usually in seven to ten days), you can use these tips to care for your body as it heals.

CHILLS   FEVER   TIREDNESS   HEADACHE

MUSCLE ACHES   COUGH   SORE THROAT   RUNNY NOSE

Hydrate, Hydrate, Hydrate

Drink plenty of fluids. Water, juice, and broth are all good options. In addition to supporting body processes like temperature regulation, brain function, and digestion, staying hydrated can decrease nasal irritation when you're sick with a virus.

Congestion Relief

Saline nasal drops and sprays can keep the passages of your nose moist and loosen mucus. If your stuffed nose is getting in the way of rest, you can also try a decongestant nasal spray. However, make sure you follow the instructions for this medicine, or else symptoms may reappear and worsen.

Rest

There are two really good reasons to rest when you're sick. The first is that your body heals better when it's under less stress. Don't try to suck it up and push through, or you'll just get sicker for longer.

The second is that colds and other viruses can easily spread. If you can, stay home from work or school and relax in bed or on the couch.

Soothe Your Throat

If you have a sore throat, you can gargle saltwater for some relief. Use one-quarter to one-half of a teaspoon (1.5 to 3 g) of salt in half a cup to a cup (120 to 230 ml) of water. You can also use lozenges or over-the-counter sprays to soothe your throat, but make sure to follow the directions closely so you don't overdo it.

Pain and Fever Relief

You can use acetaminophen and ibuprofen to reduce mild fevers and headaches. However, if your fever doesn't subside or if your temperature is 103°F (39.4°C) or higher, call a doctor.

It's best to take ibuprofen (Advil, Aleve) and aspirin with food, or they can mess with your stomach.

I HEARD THAT...

Whenever we get sick or injure ourselves, people love to chime in with treatments they swear by. But just because people have repeated things forever doesn't mean they're true. Here's what's up with a few common myths about caring for yourself.

Feed a Cold, Starve a Fever

This saying probably comes from an old belief that eating food helps the body generate warmth during a cold, and avoiding it helps the body cool down during a fever. But really, you should feed a cold **and** feed a fever. Food and water are crucial for helping your body heal. When you've got a stomach bug, focus on hydration first, then slowly incorporate bland foods like clear broths and rice back into your diet.

Vitamin C Cures Colds

Vitamin C is good for your bones, muscles, and blood vessels, but there's very little proof that it helps treat or prevent colds. In some studies, vitamin C shortened cold duration by about one day on average, but other studies showed little to no impact at all. So while it's typically safe to consume, it's not really effective at treating a cold.

The recommended daily amount of Vitamin C is 60 to 90 milligrams. More than 2,000 milligrams a day can cause health problems.

Chicken Soup Will Heal You

It may not be medicine per se, but it's true that chicken soup can make you feel better when you're sick. The broth is hydrating, the warmth can soothe a sore throat, and the seasoning can help surmount any loss of taste. Plus, the protein in chicken and carbohydrates from noodles help you feel satisfied. Vegetarian protein options like beans,  tofu, and tempeh also increase the satisfaction factor and allow you to focus on relaxation and healing.

ROCK THE KITCHEN

Looking for tips on good cooking, food storage, and cleanup you can deal with? We've got you covered! Flip through these pages for advice on treating your taste buds, making leftovers last longer, and not being that roommate who lets dishes get gross in the sink. The kitchen is nothing to fear, so look here to get inspired!

KITCHEN TOOLS

Cooking is fun, and it's cheaper than takeout. But to start, you need the right tools. With these equipment tips, no recipe will catch you off guard.

Pots and Pans

- **Nonstick pan** – Low-maintenance, easy to clean, and good for cooking almost anything. Just don't use any metal utensils on it, or you'll scratch off the nonstick coating and make the pan unsafe.

- **Soup pot** – Make soups, stocks, stews, pasta, and rice with this! You want one that can hold six quarts.

- **Dutch oven** – Great for slow cooking, deep-frying, and even baking! Careful, though—it's usually made with enameled cast iron, so it's majorly heavy.

- **Saucepan** – Use this for soups, pasta, and, uh, sauce! A three-quart saucepan is ideal when you're cooking for one.

- **Sheet pan** – A favorite for cookies and other sweet treats, and also excellent for roasting meat and vegetables.

- **Cake pan** – Use this to make cakes, loaves, casseroles—anything you don't want spilling all over the place.

Slicing and Dicing

- **Chef's knife** – Surprisingly, sharp knives are much less dangerous than dull ones. When you're cutting meat and produce, you want a blade that doesn't slip or require much force to cleanly slice.

- **Bread knife** – It's for bread! The serrated edge is perfect for slicing a loaf without crushing or tearing it. Serrated knives are also best for slicing tomatoes and layer cakes. For everything else, a chef's knife is best.

- **Cutting boards** – Don't ruin your countertops! If you need to cut anything, use one of these. You can find them in plastic and wood.

- **Can opener** – You know, for opening cans! Because nothing is more frustrating than a soup can without a pull tab.

- **Vegetable peeler** – Peel potatoes and more in a flash! You don't always need to take the skin off, but some meals just taste better with this extra step.

- **Grater** – Is that snow falling? No, it's Parmesan! You'll feel so fancy when you zest a lemon over your dessert or shred fresh cheese on your baked ziti.

Mixing and Measuring

- **Measuring cups** – You can sometimes get away with guesstimating when you're cooking, but if you do it when you bake, you'll face disaster.

- **Measuring spoons** – Perfect for oils and spices. Just don't mix up a tablespoon (Tbsp) and teaspoon (tsp).

- **Liquid measuring cup** – You can technically use standard measuring cups for liquids, but this is much easier.

- **Kitchen scale** – If you really want to be precise, and especially if you want to bake bread, use this. Measure your flour in grams, and your bread will be a slam (dunk).

- **Mixing bowls** – When you cook, you often need to do a lot of mixing at once. Get a nested set to save cupboard space.

Stirring, Flipping, and Serving

- **Spatula** – Flip pancakes and eggs with this.

- **Ladle** – Use this tool to serve soup.

- **Whisk** – Perfect for batters and gravy. It's also fun to look at.

- **Spider** – This strainer is great for pulling boiled food out of the water.

- **Colander** – Perfect for straining pasta and rinsing vegetables in your sink when needed.

- **Silicone spatula** – For all your scraping needs. This tool also helps you fold ingredients and spread frosting.

- **Tongs** – Use these to flip food in a hot oven, serve salads, or pull spaghetti out of water.

- **Cooking thermometer** – If you're cooking meat or crafting fanciful desserts, knowing the exact temperature is crucial. See this tool in action on page 35.

- **Wooden everything** – Wooden spoons and spatulas are perfect for nonstick pots and pans. They're also *so* glamorous.

HOW TO MAKE THE BEST EGGS

You can cook pretty much anything if you know your way around a stove. And eggs go with everything! How do you want 'em?

Fried

1. Heat up your pan with a little butter or olive oil. Use enough to let the egg slide around a bit.

2. Crack your egg(s) into the hot pan. Let cook until the egg white sets.

3. For sunny-side-up eggs, you're done! Otherwise, flip them and cook a few more minutes.

Scrambled

1. Crack eggs into a bowl and whip with a whisk or fork until they're airy and fully blended.

2. Heat the pan and add butter or oil. When it's hot, pour in eggs and turn the stove to medium-low.

3. Once the eggs begin to set, push them around with a spatula until they form curds. Cook until they're fluffy and warm all the way through. Ta-da!

Hardboiled

1. Put eggs in a saucepan. Add cold water until it rises about 1 inch (2.5 cm) above the eggs.

2. Bring to a boil, then turn off heat and cover the pan with a lid. Let sit for 6 to 12 minutes, depending on how firm you want the yolk. Remove the eggs and run them under cold water until they feel cool. Peel and enjoy!

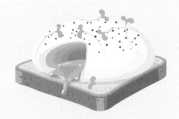

Poached

1. Put about 2 inches (5 cm) of water in a small saucepan. Add a splash of white or rice vinegar and a dash of salt.

2. Bring to a low boil and crack an egg carefully into the pan. Reduce heat to a simmer and cook for 3 to 4 minutes.

3. Remove the egg with a strainer or slotted spoon and admire your work!

Deviled

Deviled eggs are **not** Adulting 101.

CHOPPING VEGGIES

Knowing how to properly cut vegetables will do wonders for the flavor and texture of your next meal. It'll also protect your fingers!

How to Chop Vegetables

1. Place your cutting board on a flat, sturdy surface, making sure that it won't move around as you cut.

2. Use a "claw grip." With your non-dominant hand, make a claw and press your fingertips into the food you're cutting. As your food becomes smaller, curling your fingers in will help you grip the food and protect your fingers if the knife slips.

3. Stabilize your food. Always place the flat side down so that it doesn't slip while you're cutting. When cutting a round vegetable, start by cutting it in half, then place that half face-down on your cutting board.

4. Keep your knives sharp. A dull knife requires more pressure to cut, which increases the likelihood of it slipping. Take your knives to get sharpened every six months to avoid dull blades.

How to Chop an Onion

Let's test out your skills with one of the most versatile ingredients!

1. Cut half an inch (1.2 cm) away from the stem end, and just barely trim the root end.

2. From top to bottom, cut the onion in half. Place both halves flat-sides-down on the cutting board for stability (and to avoid the tear-inducing fumes).

3. Peel back the onion skin. Make lengthwise cuts into the onion, angled toward the center. The knife tip should be close to the root end, but stop short of cutting through it. Make thin or thick cuts, depending on the recipe.

4. Make crosswise cuts with your hand in the claw position. Continue moving your hand back as you cut the onion.

Why Onions Make You Cry (and What to Do About It)

When you chop an onion, you break its cell structure, releasing acids that can irritate your eyes. However, these acids are also why onions taste so good. The more you cut the onion, the more flavorful it will be. You know what they say: No pain, no gain!

However, there are a few ways to cut down on the crying:

- Use a sharp knife, and cut at an angle away from yourself.
- Chill your onions for half an hour in the freezer before slicing.
- Turn on the fan to keep vapors out of your eyes.
- Use goggles if your eyes are feeling sensitive.

COOKING MEAT

If you enjoy eating meat or want to cook for someone who does, proper preparation is essential. Bring out great flavors and prevent food poisoning with these tips.

How to Prepare Meat

1. Thaw frozen meat in the fridge for 24 hours. The fridge provides a safe temperature for thawing. After thawing, items like ground meat, stew meat, poultry, and seafood are safe for another 1 or 2 days before cooking. Red meat cuts are safe for 3 to 5 days.

2. Marinate the meat in a bowl or Ziploc bag for 15 to 20 minutes to tenderize and flavor the protein. Don't marinate for too long, or the meat will get stringy. Turn the page for more on marinades.

3. Take the meat out of the fridge about 15 to 30 minutes before cooking to make sure it cooks evenly.

4. Remove excess fat with a knife. Pull the fat taut with your non-dominant hand and slice it off in small strips. But make sure to leave some fat on the meat—the fat will render as the food cooks, making it more flavorful.

5. Season the meat right before you cook it. A bit of salt and pepper will add a great depth of flavor, and you can add other seasonings as well! (Flip to page 38 for tips.)

How to Cook Meat in the Oven

There are many ways to cook meat, but the oven is one of the easiest places to start.

1. Preheat your oven. For beef, the ideal temperature is often 325°F (165°C), and for pork and chicken, it's often 350°F (175°C). Different cuts of meat require different temperatures, so consult a recipe if you're unsure.

2. Oil a sheet pan with cooking spray or cooking oil, then lay the meat on it. Place the pan in the center rack of the oven and close the door.

3. Cook the meat until it reaches a safe internal temperature throughout. Stick a kitchen thermometer into the thickest part of the food for about 10 seconds to find out when it's ready. Below are some common cuts with the minimum internal temperature and timing.

Chicken breast – 165°F (74°C), 20 to 30 minutes

Rib roast – 145°F (63°C), 23 to 25 minutes per pound (0.45 kg)

Loin roast – 145°F (63°C), 20 minutes per pound (0.45 kg)

Let the meat rest for 10 minutes after removing it from the oven.

What's a marinade?

A marinade consists of acid, fat, salt, and flavor. It helps tenderize a cut of meat, and is the first thing that cooks when the meat hits the pan, creating a tasty crust.

Try this – olive oil, lemon juice, soy sauce, garlic, salt, and pepper
Or this – maple syrup, balsamic vinegar, and garlic powder

HOW TO MAKE RICE

If you've got a rice cooker, you can skip this page. But if you're craving a bowl of rice and don't have one, never fear! All you need is rice, a saucepan, water, and a bit of patience to get started.

How to Cook Rice

1. Measure out 1 cup (185 g) of long-grain white rice. There are thousands of varieties of rice, and they're all delicious, but this is a great type that you can find almost anywhere.

2. (Optional) Rinse your rice in a strainer under cool water for 30 seconds. Shake off the excess water. You can skip this step if you're in a rush.

3. Combine 2 cups (500 ml) of water for every 1 cup (250 ml) of rice in a saucepan. If you rinsed your rice, use 1¾ cups (425 ml) of water per 1 cup of rice instead.

4. Cover and bring to a boil. Bring the heat to medium-high.

5. Once you're at a boil, bring the heat down to medium-low and set a timer for 10 minutes. (DON'T stir the rice while it's cooking.)

6. When the rice has absorbed all the water in the pot, turn off the heat. Keep the lid on and let the rice sit for 10 more minutes. Seriously, it's worth the wait.

7. Your rice is finished! Fluff with a fork and serve.

Want to use this rice in a delicious meal? Check out page 42.

HOW TO USE SPICES

Salt and pepper are excellent seasonings for all sorts of recipes, but if you really want to step it up a notch, consider adding new spices. Use the guide below to determine which spices will enhance your next recipe! If you're having trouble imagining the flavor, dishes are included that often (though not always) feature each spice.

Allspice
- Flavor: earthy, sweet
- Mix with: cardamom, nutmeg, cinnamon, cloves, ginger
- Find me in: jerk chicken, pumpkin pie, chai latte

Basil
- Flavor: sweet, peppery
- Mix with: rosemary, thyme, oregano
- Find me in: tomato soup, pesto, caprese salad

Cardamom
- Flavor: sweet, warm
- Mix with: cinnamon, cumin, ginger, turmeric
- Find me in: palak paneer, pistachio cake, mango lassi

Cayenne Pepper
- Flavor: spicy, smoky
- Mix with: cumin, paprika, cinnamon
- Find me in: tacos, chili, hot sauce

Cinnamon
- Flavor: earthy, sweet, hot
- Mix with: allspice, cloves, nutmeg, cardamom
- Find me in: cinnamon rolls, granola, apple pie

Cloves
- Flavor: earthy, sweet
- Mix with: cinnamon, nutmeg, allspice, basil
- Find me in: honey baked ham, rice pilaf, mole sauce

Cumin
- Flavor: earthy, warm, nutty
- Mix with: cinnamon, ginger, oregano, turmeric
- Find me in: chicken tikka masala, chili, guacamole

Fennel
- Flavor: licorice-like
- Mix with: basil, cinnamon, cloves, cumin, thyme
- Find me in: Italian sausage, marinated olives, roasted salmon

Ginger

- Flavor: sweet, spicy, citrus
- Mix with: cinnamon, cloves, nutmeg, turmeric, cardamom
- Find me in: veggie stir-fry, sesame ginger salad, gingerbread cookies

Nutmeg

- Flavor: sweet, nutty, spicy
- Mix with: allspice, cloves, ginger
- Find me in: braised pork loin, white sauce, eggnog

Oregano

- Flavor: earthy
- Mix with: thyme, basil, parsley, rosemary
- Find me in: chicken oreganata, Margherita pizza, roasted asparagus

Parsley

- Flavor: bitter
- Mix with: nutmeg, basil, rosemary, thyme
- Find me in: tabbouleh, chimichurri sauce, potato salad

Paprika

- Flavor: sweet, warm
- Mix with: cardamom, cinnamon, cumin
- Find me in: chicken paprikash, paella, romesco sauce

Rosemary

- Flavor: earthy
- Mix with: oregano, thyme, basil
- Find me in: Cornish hen, roasted potatoes, focaccia

Saffron

- Flavor: bitter, sweet
- Mix with: basil, fennel, cinnamon, cloves
- Find me in: mushroom risotto, seafood pasta, saffron rice

Thyme

- Flavor: earthy
- Mix with: oregano, rosemary, basil
- Find me in: lemon chicken, mashed potatoes, roasted carrots

Turmeric

- Flavor: earthy, bitter
- Mix with: cardamom, ginger, cinnamon, cloves
- Find me in: coconut ginger soup, turmeric rice, golden lattes

HOW TO MAKE A SMOOTHIE

If you don't have time to go to the smoothie shop downtown, just open a smoothie shop in your kitchen! The only necessary elements of a smoothie are liquids and fruit. You could easily make a tasty coconut banana smoothie with, you guessed it, coconut milk and banana, but don't be afraid to pull ingredients from the other categories listed to add flavor, texture, and dare I say *aesthetics* to your favorite on-the-go treat.

LIQUID
Milk of choice
Juice of choice
Ice cream

FRUIT
Bananas
Strawberries
Raspberries
Blueberries
Avocado
Mango
Peaches

VEGETABLES
Spinach
Kale
Romaine
Pureed pumpkin
Cooked sweet potato

PROTEIN
Yogurt
Nut butter
Cottage cheese
Chia seeds
Protein powder
Silken tofu

SWEETENERS
Honey
Sugar
Dates
Chocolate
Artificial sweeteners

SPICES
Ginger
Cinnamon
Nutmeg
Cardamom
Vanilla extract
Orange extract

What order do they go in the blender?
Great question! Start with liquids, then greens, then soft ingredients (like fruits and nut butters), and finally hard ingredients (like frozen fruit). Blend until smooth.

BIG BOWL OF FOOD

A big bowl of food can be any quick and tasty meal that's easy to prepare. Salads count, but so do burrito bowls, poke bowls, noodle dishes, and more! Mix and match from the following categories for a unique and delicious meal.

BASE

Choose greens, grains, or starches to form a base for tasty flavors!

Iceberg lettuce
Baby spinach
Cabbage slaw
Rice
Noodles
Quinoa
Farro

PROTEIN

Now, toss in your protein of choice! Feel free to choose more than one. If your meat needs to be cooked first, check out page 35 for tips.

Chicken
Beef
Pork
Eggs
Tofu
Chickpeas
Salmon
Tuna
Feta cheese
Mozzarella cheese

FRUITS AND VEGETABLES

While not necessary for every dish, fruits and vegetables can add great flavor and textural variety to a meal.

Avocado	Snap peas
Mango	Edamame
Tomatoes	Orange slices
Cucumbers	Radishes
Bell peppers	Celery
Berries	Sweet potatoes
Carrots	Kale

SAUCE/ DRESSING

You can make a sauce or dressing, but feel free to buy it at the store (or your favorite restaurant). Drizzle on top and dig in!

Barbecue sauce
Hot sauce
Mayonnaise
Teriyaki sauce
French dressing
Vinaigrette
Oil of choice

CRUNCH

Garnish your dish with some flavor-packed crunch. Fresh and store-bought both work!

Raw nuts or seeds
Roasted edamame
Fried onions
Croutons
Chips

FOOD STORAGE MADE SIMPLE

All food goes bad eventually, but proper storage can help keep your food fresh until you're ready to eat it.

How to Store Leftovers

- Cool your food rapidly. To prevent bacterial growth, you want to reach a safe storage temperature of 40° F (4.4° C) or below. Divide large amounts of food into smaller portions to cool it evenly.

- Wrap your leftovers well. This helps keep bacteria out and ensures that your food will retain moisture and still taste delicious later.

- Follow time guidelines. Most leftovers can be kept in the refrigerator for 3 to 4 days or in the freezer for 3 to 4 months. Although frozen leftovers are safe indefinitely, they can lose moisture and flavor when stored longer than 4 months.

Three Ways to Thaw Frozen Leftovers

1. Thaw your leftovers in the fridge. This way takes the longest but ensures that the leftovers stay safe the entire time.

2. Thaw your leftovers in cold water. Make sure they're in a leak-proof package.

3. Thaw your leftovers in the microwave. To do this, heat your leftovers until they reach 165°F (74°C) as measured with a food thermometer.

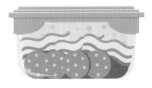

What about produce?

Fresh fruits and veggies don't need to be frozen, but they last longer and taste better when stored properly. Consult this chart to find out where to put your produce.

IN THE FRIDGE
Apples
Blueberries
Dark leafy greens
Carrots
Ginger
Broccoli

FIRST THE COUNTER, THEN THE FRIDGE WHEN RIPE
Apricots
Avocados
Mangoes
Melons
Peaches
Plums

ON THE COUNTER
Bananas
Cucumbers
Garlic
Watermelon
Zucchini
Eggplant

What about potatoes?

Store potatoes in a cool, dark place. They can last for months this way (yes, really)! Just don't keep potatoes in a plastic bag—they'll rot. Paper or mesh bags are better.

HOW TO WASH DISHES

Stuck without a dishwasher? No problem! Read ahead for tips on painless dishwashing. Then use your newfound skills to charm someone who's cooked for you (and win over your roommates). And remember, to cut down on the pile-up, wash as you go!

How to Wash Dishes (By Hand)

1. Clear your dishes of leftover food using a rubber spatula or paper towel.

2. Fill the sink with hot water and add a bit of dish soap. If there's already a big pot or bowl in the sink, clean that first and use it to hold the soapy water as you wash the rest.

3. Start by washing the cleanest items, then move on to the dirtiest. Start with glasses and flatware, then plates, bowls, and dishes, and finally any pots, pans, and cooking utensils that are still dirty.

4. Drain and refill the water as needed if it becomes greasy or dirty.

5. Place your clean dishes on a dish rack or dry them with a towel.

What shouldn't go in the dishwasher?

- Aluminum utensils
- Cast iron
- China
- Crystal
- Decorated glassware
- Plastic utensils
- Wooden utensils
- Silver

How to Wash Pots and Pans

It can seem daunting to wash these, especially when last night's dinner is stuck to them. Follow these steps to get your pots and pans sparkling in no time.

1. Scrape leftover food out with a rubber spatula or paper towel.

2. Soak cookware before you start washing. Add detergent or baking soda to the pot or pan and fill with hot water. Then leave to soak for 15 to 30 minutes.

3. Drain, then clean as usual. If food is still stuck to your dishes, scour gently with the rough side of your sponge.

Still didn't work? Bring a solution of baking soda and water (3 tablespoons to 1 quart) to a boil in the pan. Take it off the heat, add a bit of dish soap, and allow it to cool. Then clean as usual.

What can I pour down the drain?

Unless you have a garbage disposal, most things can't go down the drain. (Well, they technically can, but you'll regret it.) However, a few things can go down the drain without messing up your plumbing, like milk, tea, and coffee (no grounds!).

If you do have a garbage disposal (ooh, fancy!), there are still a few things it can't handle well, including bones, nuts and shells, bread, seeds, stringy veggies, grease, and anything that isn't food.

CHEAP FOOD HACKS

Who said growing up meant you had to stop eating what you like? Use these quick tips to hack your favorite cheap eats.

Boxed Mac & Cheese

You can eat it as is, but if you're feeling adventurous, try any of the following additions to step it up a notch.

- Add actual cheese. Mozzarella adds stretch, gruyere adds sweet and savory notes, and parmesan adds some saltiness.
- Use Greek yogurt instead of milk for a tangy flavor.
- Add roasted vegetables. Sometimes it's just easier to eat veggies when they're covered in cheese. Roasted broccoli adds a delicious crunch.
- Mash in avocado with the sauce. Green equals healthy, right?

Instant Ramen

Ahh, instant ramen. It's under a dollar and packed with flavor. Use these to make it even better.

- Add an egg. Fried, hardboiled, or poached eggs will boost the protein and add some delicious flavor. Check out page 31 for tips!
- Throw some crunch on top! Onion flakes, sesame seeds, and dried seaweed all taste delicious and add textural variety.
- Add fresh aromatics: garlic, ginger, and green onions (scallions). These create great flavor and smell!
- Buff up the broth with soy sauce, sesame oil, and/or chili paste (all cheap at the store).

ADULTING AT HOME

Whether it's a dorm, an apartment, or a room at your parents' home, your living space can have a huge effect on your mood. Yes, it's a rip-off to have to do laundry when you're going to end up with more laundry tomorrow. But most household stuff isn't that bad once you get started. The reward of clean, comfy clothes will be worth it!

WASHING YOUR CLOTHES

Giving your clothes some love and attention will help keep them in top shape. For a low-stress laundry experience, try these tips.

- **Check the labels on your clothes.** Instructions like "tumble dry low" and "hand wash only" are more than just suggestions—taking shortcuts will wear out your clothes faster.

- **Sort your laundry.** Separate light and dark clothes to prevent dyes from ruining your whites.

- **Choose any all-purpose laundry detergent.** No need to spend extra on "premium" detergent or a top-shelf brand.

- **Pick the right water temperature and cycle.** You can wash most things in cold water. Save warm water for bed linens, towels, socks, and underwear, which are prone to heavy soiling.

- **Check the pockets of your clothes to save your stuff.** Make sure all zippers are zipped, and all buttons are buttoned up. Pretreat any stains you see (turn the page for more info).

- **Place delicate items in mesh bags before you put them in the wash.** It'll help them keep their shape in the machine.

- **Don't overload the washer!** It's bad for the machine and won't get your laundry as clean. Two loads are better than one.

- **Take your clothes out fast when finished to avoid wrinkles and mildew.** You can hang dry your clothes or place them in the dryer. If you use a front-loading washer, wipe the seal and leave the door open after every wash to help stop mold.

Machine Settings

Normal

PURPOSE:

Removes stains and dirt from relatively durable fabric

USE FOR:

Cotton, linen, durable synthetics

Permanent Press

PURPOSE:

Shorter than the Normal cycle, uses warm water with a lower spin for a gentler wash

USE FOR:

Synthetics, semi-synthetics, blends, clothes that wrinkle easily

Delicates

PURPOSE:

Uses cold or warm water with low to no spin for delicate items

USE FOR:

Silk, wool, delicate synthetics

Rinse & Spin

PURPOSE:

Quickly rinses and removes moisture, uses no detergent

USE FOR:

Bathing suits

Speed Wash

PURPOSE:

A fast cycle for a few lightly soiled items

USE FOR:

Relatively durable clothes you need to wear soon

Heavy Duty

PURPOSE:

A long warm or hot wash and high-speed tumbling to remove dirt

USE FOR:

Towels, jeans, heavily soiled items

TREATING STAINS

Your favorite shirt was just doused in ketchup! You put on your pants only to find some mystery stain on the ankle! A baby threw up on your shoulder (yuck)! Whatever the cause, stains throw us into chaos mode. But by following some simple steps, your clothes can look good as new in no time.

General Tips

- Deal with the stain as soon as possible. The less time it has to set, the easier it will be to remove.

- Pretreat the item with a stain remover before washing.

- Wash according to tag instructions. Don't put anything in the dryer until the stain has been removed.

What about stains from...

ADHESIVES?

1. Apply ice or cold water to the item, then scrape with a dull knife.

2. Apply a prewash stain remover.

3. Rinse, then wash.

BABY FORMULA?

1. Pretreat stain with a product containing enzymes.

2. Soak for at least 30 minutes (and up to several hours) for old stains.

3. Wash.

BARBECUE SAUCE?

1. From the back of the stain, rinse with cold water.

2. Pretreat the stain with liquid laundry detergent, brushing with a soft brush.

3. Rinse well. Then sponge the stain with white vinegar and rinse again.

4. Repeat steps 2 and 3 until the stain is mostly removed.

5. Use a prewash stain remover. Then wash. Use bleach if it's safe for the fabric.

BEVERAGES?

1. Soak the stain in cool water.

2. Pretreat the stain with a prewash stain remover or liquid laundry detergent.

3. Wash. Use bleach if it's safe for the fabric.

BLOOD (FRESH)?

1. Soak in cold water. Hot water will set blood stains.

2. Wash as usual.

BLOOD (DRIED)?

1. Pretreat with a stain remover or soak in warm water with a product containing enzymes.

2. Wash as usual.

BODILY FLUIDS?

1. Pretreat with a stain remover or soak in a product containing enzymes.

2. Wash. Use bleach if it's safe for the fabric.

DRYING YOUR CLOTHES

Using a dryer is no sweat. For the opposite of a rough-and-tumble experience, check out the tips below.

Separate clothes that need air-drying from clothes that don't.

Untangle your wet clothes. Tangled items may not fully dry. Give shirts a firm shake to help with wrinkles.

Use mesh bags for delicate items. Do NOT put underwire bras in the dryer. Air-dry them if you want them to live.

Use dryer sheets. They help reduce static cling and soften fabric.

Do multiple loads if you have a lot of items.

Select the right drying temperature and setting. Check the guide if you're unsure.

Select a drying time if the dryer doesn't self-select one. Small loads will take about half an hour to dry, and larger loads can take up to an hour.

Remove and fold your clothes as soon as the cycle is done to prevent wrinkles. Turn the page for more information.

Clean the lint trap! It's not just about how well the dryer will work— it's also a fire hazard. It takes like two seconds.

Machine Settings

Air Fluff

PURPOSE:

Uses no heat by drawing room temperature air to remove dust and fluff garments

USE FOR:

Items that are already dry (great for blankets)

Delicate

PURPOSE:

Uses low heat to protect delicate garments

USE FOR:

Activewear, loosely woven garments, silk, embroidered fabrics

Permanent Press/Wrinkle-Resistant

PURPOSE:

Uses medium heat and stops generating heat during the last several minutes of drying time to minimize wrinkles

USE FOR:

Most everyday clothing items, fabrics that wrinkle easily, synthetics

Regular

PURPOSE:

Uses high heat to quickly dry clothes

USE FOR:

Strong cottons and other durable fabrics

Steam

PURPOSE:

Generates steam within the dryer to remove wrinkles from garments; can't dry freshly washed clothes

USE FOR:

Wrinkled fabrics that require a refresh

HAND-WASHING AND AIR-DRYING

Hand-washing and air-drying your clothes is not only good for delicate fabrics, it's also pretty easy! Instead of never wearing special items or damaging them in the washing machine, use these techniques to clean them safely.

How to Hand-Wash Your Clothes

1. Read the label to see what detergent is recommended. When in doubt, choose a mild one.

2. Fill a tub or sink with water and add about a teaspoon of detergent. Use cool water if a temperature isn't specified on the label.

3. Submerge the garment and soak. Gently move it through the water.

4. Drain the sink or tub, and refill it with cool, clean water. Gently move the garment around in the water until all the soap is removed.

5. Hang the garment to dry. Repeat steps 1 through 4 for any other items.

Clothes You Need to Air-Dry (Yes, Really.)

- **Athletic wear** – Spandex and elastic lose their stretch in the dryer. Don't ruin your leggings.

- **Wool** – That beautiful sweater your grandmother made you? It will be destroyed in the dryer. Lay it flat to dry.

- **Denim** – Only put your jeans in the dryer if you want them to shrink. Otherwise, air-dry them.

- **Undergarments** – Bras need to be hand-washed and air-dried. Lay them flat to dry.

- **Anything hand-washed** – If it's too delicate to put in the washing machine, it's for sure too delicate to put in the dryer. Play it safe, kid.

Tips for Drying Clothes Indoors

- Sweaters and heavy garments should be laid flat to dry (not in a pile).

- Other garments can be hung using hangers or a drying rack.

EASY MODE: FOLDING YOUR CLOTHES

T-shirts

1. Lay the T-shirt on a flat surface.

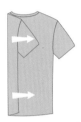

2. Fold each side toward the center.

3. If the shirt has long sleeves, fold each sleeve back over itself.

4. Fold the shirt in half from hem to neck. Voilà!

What about sweaters?

You can fold a sweater just like a T-shirt! But if you're low on space, after folding in the arms, roll up the sweater from hem to neck to save space. Just don't roll it too tightly—it will stretch if you do!

Dress Shirts

Hang dress shirts when you're at home. When you travel, use these tips to skip wrinkles and rips.

1. Button up the shirt from top to bottom.

2. Lay the shirt on a flat surface, front side down.

3. Fold one sleeve along the crease where it meets the shoulder. Then fold it back on top of itself so that the sleeve is aligned with the edge of the shirt.

4. Repeat with the other sleeve so that the sleeves are on top of one another.

5. Fold the bottom of the shirt upward toward the collar. Perfect!

HARD MODE: FOLDING A FITTED SHEET

1. Holding your fitted sheet lengthwise, find all four corners.

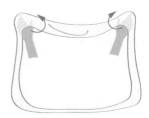

2. Place each hand inside the top two longest corners at the seams. The opening should be facing your body.

3. Grab the corners and flip them inside out. Then switch your hands and place them both back inside the corners.

4. Bring your right hand to your left hand so that the two corners are touching. Then flip the right corner over the left corner so that everything is hanging from your left hand.

5. Swap hands again so that the two corners are hanging from your right hand. Use your left hand to grab the final corner.

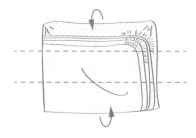 

6. Place the sheet onto a flat surface, with the elastic facing up. The elastic of your sheet should look like a U shape.

7. Fold from the top of the sheet down into thirds until you've got a long rectangle. Then flip it over and fold into thirds horizontally.

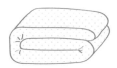

8. You're done! Congratulations— you've mastered adulting.

HOW TO CLEAN YOUR ROOM FAST

A neat bedroom makes you feel good and offers a more welcoming space when you have friends over. Call it a pointless struggle against entropy if you want, but if you made it to page 62 of this book, you might as well give it a try.

Easy Cleaning Tips

- **Start with your clothes.** Pick up all the clothing on your floor (and bed) and decide if it's dirty or clean. Dirty clothes go in the hamper to be washed (page 50), and clean clothes get folded and put away (page 58).

- **Remove the dirty dishes.** Eating in bed is a blast, but crusty bowls and nasty smells are no fun, and crumbs attract bugs. Take those dishes to the kitchen for cleaning (page 46).

- **Throw out the trash.** Similar to organizing your clothes, decide if something is important or if it's trash. Important stuff goes in one pile, garbage goes in a trash bag. Once you've taken care of the garbage, put the objects back in their rightful places. Books on the bookshelf, papers in the desk drawer, pillows on the bed.

Before

Want to take it a step further?

Dust and vacuum. Take out a paper towel or that weird feathery thing in the closet and lightly brush the surfaces of your room to remove dust. When you're done, sweep or vacuum the floor for maximum cleanliness.

How to Make Your Bed (the Easy Way)

1. Place the fitted sheet on top of your mattress, pulling each corner of the sheet over each corner of your mattress. (If it doesn't seem to fit, it may be oriented wrong. Try rotating it 90 degrees.) Then, lay the flat sheet evenly on your bed.

2. If you're feeling fancy, fold the sides and bottom of the top sheet under the mattress.

3. Lay your comforter, quilt, or duvet on top of your bedding. Fold the edges under your mattress or leave them loose depending on your preference.

4. Place your sleeping pillows on top, and fluff them by grabbing both sides and squeezing them together.

5. If you have them, add throw pillows in front of your sleeping pillows. And done!

REDUCE, REUSE, RECYCLE

We can all do our part to lessen our environmental footprint. These tips are as true today as they were in the '90s.

Reduce

Create less waste in the first place! Cut down on single-use plastics by carrying a reusable water bottle, taking reusable bags to the store, and finding out how many foods and household liquids you can refill in bulk containers.

Reuse

On top of using durable bottles and reusable bags, make the most of what's already out there before you buy new. A kitchen utensil you got secondhand for four dollars is better for the environment than any newly manufactured "green" one.

Recycle

Reducing and reusing are the most important things you can do, especially since a lot of what we recycle ends up trashed anyway. However, when you really can't reuse anymore, recycling is the next best thing. So when you do add items to the waste stream, find out first whether or not they can be recycled.

Should I recycle?

Paper?
Yes, if it's...

Newspaper

Junk mail

Scrap paper

Paper bags

Paperback books

Metal?
Yes, if it's...

Aluminum, steel, and tin cans

Empty paint and aerosol cans

Aluminum baking dishes

Plastic?
Yes, if it's...

Food containers

Bottles

Jars

Shampoo and detergent bottles

Spray bottles

Glass?
Yes, if it's...

Bottles and jars

Cardboard?
Yes, if it's...

Corrugated cardboard boxes

Clean pizza boxes

Paper towel rolls

Egg cartons (not foam or plastic)

Dry food and shipping boxes

What NOT to recycle

Plastic bags

Metal hangers

Flammables

Needles and syringes

Clothing and bedding

Light bulbs

Tissues, paper towels, and napkins

Pots and pans

Disposable plates, cups, and takeout containers

HOW TO COPE WITH A TOILET

You use it every day, yet you probably spend as little time thinking about it as humanly possible. But here's the truth: Absolutely nothing about cleaning a toilet is worse than seeing a gross bowl before you sit down. Try this quick and simple process now, and feel better about it forever.

Toilet Cleaning Supplies

- Rubber gloves
- Scrub sponge
- Toilet cleaner* or vinegar
- Toilet brush
- All-purpose disinfectant
- Paper towels
- Pumice stone (optional, for heavy stains)

How to Clean a Toilet

1. Apply toilet cleaner (or a cup of vinegar) to the bowl and allow it to soak. Quickly swish the cleaner around the bowl with a brush.

2. While the cleaner soaks, spray the toilet exterior with an all-purpose disinfectant.

3. Use a scrub sponge to clean the outside of the toilet.

4. Use a toilet brush to clean the bowl. If you have hard water rings or stains, you can use a pumice stone to remove them. That wasn't so bad, right?

*If you have a dog or cat, and you use toilet cleaner, make sure your pet doesn't drink from the toilet while it's got chemicals in it.

How to Plunge a Toilet

Don't panic. Clogs happen to everyone.

1. Turn off the water to prevent any more overflow. There's a knob at the base of the toilet.

2. Hold the handle of the plunger and put the bell into the toilet bowl so that it covers the drain opening.

3. Push down gently to force the air out of the bell to create a vacuum.

4. Plunge in and out vigorously, maintaining the seal. This will force water in both directions in the drain, which will loosen most clogs.

5. Continue plunging until the clog is dislodged. Turn the water on and flush again to reveal a working toilet.

How to Clean a Toilet Brush

Ugh, I know. You can do it.

1. After you've finished cleaning, rinse the toilet brush in water. Then spray the brush head generously with disinfectant spray.

2. Wipe down the handle with a disinfectant wipe, and use a second disinfectant wipe to clean the inside of the holder. Keep the surfaces wet for at least ten minutes.

3. Dry the holder with a microfiber cloth. Allow the brush to air-dry before putting it back in the holder. Until next time, toilet brush.

HOW TO MAKE YOUR BATHROOM SPARKLE

Another thing that feels much worse when you're dreading it than when you're actually doing it.

Sink

1. Spray a general disinfectant around the bathroom sink. Then wipe with a cloth or sponge.

2. Spray faucet handles with a disinfectant spray. Wait a bit (check the package for how long), then wipe down.

Floor

1. Remove any loose objects from the ground. If you have a bath mat, you can either remove it or wash it.

2. Use a broom to sweep up dust from the floor.

3. Fill a bucket with warm water and mix in a floor-safe cleaner. Clean the floor with a mop.

4. Rinse the floor with a slightly wet mop. Then dry the floor with a clean towel to avoid any mold growth or mildew.

Tub

1. Remove and wipe down everything in the tub to avoid getting cleaning products on your stuff.

2. Clear out the drain by pouring half a cup of baking soda down the drain, followed by half a cup of distilled white vinegar. Wait a few minutes, then flush it with hot water.

3. Apply all-purpose cleaner or tub cleaner to the inside of the tub. Let it sit for about five minutes, then wipe down the tub. Rinse well.

4. Clean soap scum with a toothbrush. (Not one you use for your teeth!) Tough stains may require a scrub brush and cleanser. Rinse again after using these.

5. Wipe down everything with a clean towel. Did your tub always sparkle like that?

Standing Shower

1. Remove everything from the shower and wipe down each item with a wet cloth.

2. Turn on the bathroom fan and open the doors or windows to ventilate the room. Then use a shower head or bucket to wet the tile walls of the shower.

3. Remove mildew with a solution of one part chlorine bleach and two parts water. Apply with a sponge (and wear gloves!), and let sit for ten minutes. Then scrub with an old toothbrush and rinse with hot water.

4. Spray a cleaning solution on the walls and floor of the shower, and leave for ten minutes. Then scrub with a sponge or plastic mesh scrubber.

5. Rinse with clean water and use a squeegee or old towel to dry. You deserve a long shower after all that.

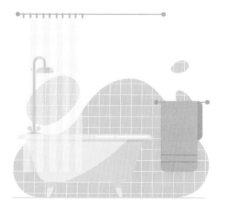

SEWING BY HAND

Knowing some simple sewing can be super helpful in a pinch. If you lose a button, get a tear in your clothing, or notice a loose thread, you'll be up to the job with these tips. You can get small sewing kits at most convenience stores if you don't already have a needle and thread lying around.

How to Thread a Needle

1. Unspool about 2 feet (60 cm) of thread and cut it.

2. Use scissors to cut off the tip of one end of the thread so that the edge is clean.

3. Insert the thread through the eye of the needle. If you're having difficulty, you can lick the end of the thread. You can also hold the needle above a white cloth or sheet of paper to make the hole look bigger.

4. Pull the thread through the needle to create a tail. You want it to be at least 2 inches long so that the thread won't slip back out of the needle as you work. You can also double up the thread all the way to the end and then knot it to create a stronger seam.

5. Tie a knot at the end of the thread (not the tail). This will secure your thread as you sew. Double the knot if the fabric has a loose weave.

SINGLE THREAD   DOUBLE THREAD

How to Sew a Running Stitch

1. Thread your needle, estimating how much thread you will need for your project. You typically need about two and a half times the length of what you'll sew.

2. Pull the needle through the "wrong" side of the fabric (the side that won't be facing outward) and come up to the top side. Continue to pull gently until the knot you tied is snug against the wrong side.

3. Push the needle back down through the fabric a short distance away. Continue to pull the thread through until there's no loose excess on the top side on the fabric. Don't pull so hard that the fabric puckers. Congratulations—you've made a stitch!

4. Pull the needle through the wrong side of the fabric through to the top again, the same distance as your first stitch. To help keep stitches even, imagine the length of the stitch as a physical object. Some people picture a grain of rice for each stitch.

5. Repeat until you're finished! Tie a knot on the wrong side of the fabric, and admire your work!

MENDING YOUR CLOTHES

Before you throw away a worn-out shirt or pair of pants, ask yourself, "Is there really nothing I can do to fix this?" Some clothes might have to go, but knowing some quick fixes will reduce waste, save your wallet, and keep your clothes looking good longer.

How to Patch Your Jeans

1. Get a denim patch. These can be found at stores, or you can make your own by cutting out a patch from an old pair of jeans that is slightly larger than the hole you're mending. You can also use other fabric if you want some fun contrast!

2. If you have an iron-on patch, use an iron to affix the patch to the hole on the right side of the denim.

3. If you don't have an iron-on patch, turn your jeans inside out, and lay the patch over the hole.

4. Thread a needle, then stitch around the hole about half an inch (1.2 cm) away from the patch's edge. You can use the running stitch illustrated on the previous page.

5. Turn your jeans right side out, and you're done!

How to Sew a Button

1. Thread your needle with strong thread. If you don't have strong thread, you can double up the thread through the needle.

2. Position the button on the fabric. Then push the threaded needle up through the fabric and through one of the buttonholes. Pull the thread all the way through.

3. Push the needle through another buttonhole, down to the wrong side of the fabric. Again, pull the thread all the way through.

4. Continue this process until the button is secure. This may mean sewing through all of the button's holes a couple of times. If there are four holes, sew diagonally across the holes to make an X pattern.

5. When you're finished, push the thread through to the wrong side of the fabric and tie a knot to finish it.

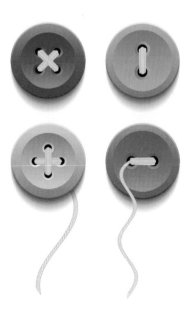

ULTIMATE TOOLBOX GUIDE

Be prepared for any home-improvement adventure with these in your toolbox.

- **Adjustable wrench** – Tighten and loosen nuts, bolts, and plumbing fixtures. Please turn off the water first.

- **Flathead screwdriver** – Has a flat-bladed tip. Use it for (almost) anything!

- **Phillips-head screwdriver** – Has a four-pointed star shape at the end. Use it for tough (and tiny) screws.

- **Claw hammer** – Use one end to drive nails in, and the claw to pull nails out.

- **Pliers** – Perfect for gripping, bending, and cutting. Use for all your wire needs.

- **Tape measure** – Measure furniture, walls, and projects. Perfect for measuring nonrefundable décor before you buy it.

- **Level** – Helps you hang stuff straight. No more crooked mirrors or haunted portraits!

- **Utility knife** – Perfect for cutting zip ties, stripping wire, and opening that sweet new pair of sneakers.

- **Flashlight** – You know, for light! You might need it when changing a tire. (For more on that, check out page 146.)

- **Electric drill** – Like a regular drill, but faster! Some even come with attachments for sanding and stirring.

- **Stud finder** – Use before hanging things, or you will absolutely wreck the drywall.

- **Wood glue** – You know, for wood! Regular glue won't cut it.

- **Safety goggles** – You know, for your eyes! Begone, dust and other dangerous substances.

- **Work gloves** – You know, for your hands! Protect them from injury and chemicals.

- **Duct tape** – Not just for sick jewelry, this is also perfect for temporary repairs.

It's handy to have some nails, screws, and sandpaper on hand for quick projects.

HOW TO CHANGE A LIGHT BULB

1. Turn off power to the socket by flipping off the wall switch or unplugging the light fixture. That way you won't shock yourself. Make sure to wait a minute to let the light bulb cool.

2. If it's a ceiling light, find a secure stool (no wobbly chairs or tables) to stand on.

3. Remove the old bulb. Gently grab it and loosen the bulb by turning it to the left.

4. Put in a new bulb with a matching wattage (you can check this on the surface of the old bulb) by screwing it into the socket.

5. Turn the lights back on and dispose of the old bulb. Make sure to wrap up the old bulb in a bag or old newspaper so it doesn't shatter. Easy!

Watts vs. Lumens

Watts (W) measure electricity usage. Light fixtures have wattage recommendations because that flow of electricity creates heat, so using the incorrect wattage can cause wire damage and create a fire hazard.

Lumens measure brightness. Wattage does not always correlate with the amount of light emitted, so check the box for the number of lumens if you're looking to really brighten a room.

What are LEDs?

LEDs (light-emitting diodes) are considered to be very energy-efficient, because they can achieve a very high brightness with fewer watts. Because of this, they also tend to last longer than other light bulbs.

However, there's no wrong light bulb to choose—any kind will do the job!

FEELINGS, FRIENDSHIP, AND FUN

We all need to feel loved and supported. Sometimes, taking care of the people you love can be a big job, and so can taking care of yourself. But you don't have to go it alone.

KNOWING WHAT YOU'RE FEELING

Sometimes it's easy to know how you're feeling—what activities you enjoy, or what gets on your nerves. But other times, emotions sneak up on you until they're suddenly too much to handle. Your feelings aren't "wrong," even when they're huge and uncomfortable and weird. If you do ever feel overwhelmed by them, you might find some of the strategies below helpful for meeting them with curiosity and compassion.

Name Your Feelings

All of them! As you go about your day, consciously name how certain things make you feel—annoyed, flattered, nervous, whatever. Over time, you'll start to recognize which events trigger specific emotions. Sometimes just putting a name to a feeling makes it easier to observe and helps you put it in perspective.

Track an Emotion

Pick a feeling and track it—how often you feel it, how strong the feeling is. Mark it down on a checklist, or a color tracker if you feel artistic. (You can find some examples of mood charts online.) Try it for a day, a week, or a month, and see if any patterns pop up.

Keep a Journal

Take some time each morning or evening to write about what's going on and how you feel about it. You don't need to start with a plan or a structure for your writing. Just begin, and let it all out on the page. A lot of thoughts and feelings that seem muddy may reveal themselves along the way.

Locate Your Feelings

Feelings can take over your body. In fact, it can almost feel like they have bodies of their own. You experience a certain emotion and your whole body shifts. That can make it hard to talk about how you're feeling, because it's as if the feeling itself is doing all the talking. This is where it helps to get curious. Before a confrontation, try asking yourself these questions:

- Where, in my body, is this feeling located?

- If this feeling had a name, what would it be? Think about how anger is a broad category of different named experiences (annoyance, frustration, bitterness, fury, etc.). Which one is appearing to you?

- What does this feeling want? What is it responding to?

It can be sort of weird to treat emotions like this, but it can also lead to some interesting discoveries about your needs and your values. Then, when you do face a conflict with someone else (like on page 92), your feelings can guide you instead of speaking for you.

HOW TO RELAX

Maybe you have a big exam coming up or a million things to get done. Maybe your friends are really getting on your nerves or said something that hurt you. Maybe you're not sure why, but you wake up in the morning feeling completely on edge. Whatever the reason, when you're finding it hard to chill out, give these tips a shot.

Short-Term Relief

- Practice deep breathing. Find a quiet place and put your hands on your belly. Breathe in slowly through your nose to the count of three, then breathe out slowly through your mouth to the same count. Continue until you feel more centered.

- Release the tension in your body. Find a quiet place and sit or lie down. Inhale and tense your muscles for a few seconds, then exhale and let them relax. Focus on one area of your body at a time, starting at your toes and slowly moving up to your head.

- Write down what you're feeling. Once it's on paper, it'll take up less space in your head. For some added relief, you can tear up the paper when you're done.

- Find your peaceful place. When you're alone, think about a place, real or imagined, that brings you joy. Imagine the details of that place—sights, sounds, tastes, and tactile elements. Continue until this location is clear in your mind. Now, whenever you feel overwhelmed, close your eyes and return to this place to calm your mind and body.

Long-Term Help

- **Identify what upsets you.** Are there particular classes or aspects of work that cause a lot of anxiety? Are there people who make you feel angry? Do you feel different when you drink caffeine? By knowing what people, events, or objects set you off, you can take time to prepare coping strategies or limit your exposure.

- **Consider talking to a therapist or counselor.** You deserve a place to talk about your problems, no matter how big or how small. Go to page 84 for more info.

- **Practice meditation.** When done regularly, meditation can help you calm your body and your brain, in both moments of crisis and the long term. For more on how to meditate, turn the page.

HOW TO MEDITATE

Meditation is a simple way to reduce stress and calm your body. There are many different ways to practice meditation, but if you're not sure where to begin, start here!

Let's Get Started!

1. Choose a quiet, relaxed environment, and wear comfortable clothes. You can play calm music or white noise if you like. Try going to:

    - Your bedroom
    - An outdoor space
    - A walk-in closet

2. Decide how long you'd like to meditate. Some people spend up to half an hour meditating, but you can start with just five minutes.

3. Stretch before you begin to release tension from your body.

4. Find a comfortable position: sitting, lying down, or even standing. Let your spine be straight and your neck free of tension.

5. Close your eyes and focus on your breathing. You can use a mental image to guide your breathing, like an ocean wave rising and falling or a leaf bobbing up and down on the wind.

6. If your mind wanders, return to your breathing. Imagine each thought that comes into your head as a passing train, bird, or butterfly. You don't need to judge or "solve" your thoughts, and you don't have to sit with them, either. Acknowledge them, then let them go.

7. Continue until your time is up. How do you feel?

Some Tips

- Try to meditate at around the same time each day. You'll get the most out of it if you make it part of a routine.

- Look for guided meditations, either in person or online. They can help you practice different styles of meditation and explore which ones work well for you.

What about yoga?

Yoga is not only excellent exercise, but can also promote a sense of calm through physical movement, deep breathing, and concentration. If you find you prefer class environments, or even if you're just looking for some movement to practice in addition to meditation, yoga is a great option!

REACHING OUT

Sometimes, feelings, events, and relationships become too much to handle on your own. And while it's good to talk to friends and trusted adults, it can also be helpful to speak to a professional. A good therapist can make space to listen to you, then help you sort through what you're dealing with and find coping strategies that work for you. If you feel like this might be a good step for you, use the following tips to guide your search.

What You Want

Many therapists specialize in different areas, like depression, anxiety, or PTSD. Think about what your goals might be when you're looking for a therapist or psychiatrist, or both. It's okay if what you want or need changes over time—it doesn't have to be set in stone for you to reach out.

Culture and Identity

What you need from a professional may look different than what someone else needs, especially when it comes to your identity and background. You can ask trusted friends and community members for references, and you can search online for therapists who have experience working with communities you are part of.

Style and Approach

There are tons of different therapeutic approaches that offer unique ways of dealing with your inner world and life experiences. You may find that certain styles appeal to you more than others, which can help you focus your search. Don't be afraid to test out different approaches. You're not locked into one style just because it's what you've been doing.

Insurance Coverage

Not every therapist will be covered by insurance (for more on that, check out page 126), so reach out to your provider to see what kind of care is covered. Some resources may not be covered outright but can be reimbursed (with some annoying paperwork), so it's good to check before setting up an appointment.

Interviews

Yes, you can totally interview your therapist! Not everyone is going to be the right fit, and that's okay. Many professionals offer free consultations. Ask questions about their process, their specialties, and whatever else is important to you. You want to work with someone you can trust. If the energy feels off, that's enough of a reason to move on to another option!

There are several types of mental health professionals. Here's a quick cheat sheet to the most common ones.

Therapist: Someone who is licensed to provide talk therapy, including counselors, clinical social workers, and many psychologists.

Psychiatrist: A medical doctor who can prescribe medication for mental health issues. Some psychiatrists also provide talk therapy.

Psychiatric Nurse Practitioner: A nurse trained in psychiatry. Can prescribe medications in some states.

Many people see both a therapist for talk therapy and, if needed, a psychiatrist for medication.

MAKING FRIENDS

Sometimes it's as simple as saying "hi" to someone sitting near you. But when it's not that simple, try this.

How to Meet People

- Join a group. If you can't find one that fits your interests through school or work, look online or in your local cafés and libraries to find some groups or clubs to join.

- Volunteer. Volunteering not only helps those around you, but also allows you to connect with people who share your values.

- Look online. You can find people from all over the world who share your interests and make you feel a little less alone. Just remember to be careful with your personal information, and that you can always block people or leave groups if they make you feel bad.

How to Make Friends

- Take initiative. If you're too anxious to message first, and the person you want to be friends with is also too anxious to message first, you'll never talk! Just reach out to say hi and go from there.

- Listen and share. Ask your friends about their interests and what's going on with them, and let them get to know you, too.

- Practice kindness. Small gestures can let someone know you care. If you think someone has cool shoes or tells good jokes, just tell them! It'll make their day. (You can learn more about great compliments on page 96.)

- Stay in touch. If you enjoy spending time with someone, make plans to do so again. If you're not sure what to do, check out the boredom-busting activities on the next page. And even if it's been a while since you and a friend were in touch, check in. They'll love hearing from you.

FINDING SOMETHING TO DO

There's always something to do—it's just hard to think of it in the moment when you're feeling incurably bored. Check out this list of fifty boredom-destroying activities to tackle on your own or with a pal.

- ☐ Go to the movies
- ☐ Check out local museums
- ☐ Take a virtual museum tour
- ☐ Fill in a coloring book
- ☐ Create a time capsule
- ☐ Clear your closet
- ☐ Write out your goals
- ☐ Read a book
- ☐ Binge-watch a new series
- ☐ Practice a new hobby
- ☐ Take a quick walk
- ☐ Do an at-home workout
- ☐ Call a friend or family member
- ☐ Take a nap
- ☐ Test out a recipe
- ☐ Make a gratitude list
- ☐ Do a puzzle
- ☐ Write a short story or poem
- ☐ Fill out a crossword
- ☐ Write a letter (to anyone!)
- ☐ Play a new video game
- ☐ Host a virtual meetup
- ☐ Paint a picture
- ☐ Learn calligraphy
- ☐ Put together a birthday/holiday wish list
- ☐ Make a care package
- ☐ Do karaoke (at home or out)
- ☐ Have a spa day
- ☐ Practice meditation
- ☐ Look through old photo albums
- ☐ Clean your sneakers
- ☐ Go stargazing
- ☐ Try to break a world record
- ☐ Plant some seeds
- ☐ Track your ancestry
- ☐ Drive to the beach
- ☐ Go for a hike (plan one on page 158)
- ☐ Tie-dye your clothes
- ☐ Learn a language
- ☐ Make a playlist
- ☐ Watch a classic movie
- ☐ Interview your family members
- ☐ Play some minigolf
- ☐ Learn how to juggle
- ☐ Make homemade ice cream
- ☐ Sew something (page 70, anyone?)
- ☐ Listen to a new radio station
- ☐ Visit an arcade
- ☐ Go bowling
- ☐ Make paper airplanes

PICKING PERFECT GIFTS

From best friends' birthdays to awkward Secret Santas, it feels good to make someone smile. Don't be daunted by the job—just ask these questions to figure out something they'll love.

How do they spend their time?

Think about their interests and look for gifts in that field. Maybe your writer friend wants a new journal, or your painterly dad could use a new brush set or canvas. A gift tailored to someone's hobbies will show you care.

What are they drawn to?

If your giftee often wears/uses a certain brand or buys merch from a favorite band, chances are they'll enjoy more of it. See if there's anything in your price range that goes with other clothes or items your giftee has.

What might they want to learn?

If your giftee has mentioned wanting to learn a new language, skill, or craft, you can give them the opportunity! Online or in-person classes and work-shops can make a great gift. Maybe you can even take a class together.

How do they relax?

Do they like bad reality TV? Or relaxing with a face mask and a scented candle? Whether it's going to the gym or eating fancy-schmancy ice cream, knowing how someone chills out after a stressful day may help you procure a perfect gift.

What can you do together?

Sometimes the best gift is quality time! Take a hike somewhere new, share a meal, or see a movie together. Just hanging out is a lovely, affordable, lasting way to make memories, trusted by adults and teens since forever.

When in Doubt, Try This

If you're really stumped, these will please just about anyone!

- Home-baked treats
- A gift card to a movie theater or restaurant
- A thoughtful letter or creative card

Gifting Your Time

While it doesn't exactly work for birthdays or holidays, gifting your time to a friend is a great way of showing you care. Here are some things you can do that someone might appreciate (just make sure to ask if it's wanted first):

- Walk their dog
- Cook them a meal
- Take on a chore
- Run some errands
- Teach a skill

WRITING THANK YOU NOTES

Breeze through any notes life calls you to write with this quick guide.

For Gifts

Use details about the gift (what you like about it, how you'll use it, and how it made you feel) to write something from the heart.

Thank you so much for the quilt! I love the green and blue color scheme—it matches my bedroom perfectly. I know you spent so much time working on it, and the thought and care you put into it means so much to me. Thank you again.

For Help

When thanking someone for doing you a favor, or being there for you during a tough time, think about how you were helped and what it meant to you before sitting down to write.

I just wanted to reach out and thank you for watching my cat last weekend! When I had to travel home last-minute, I was so worried about Socks, and it really eased my mind to have you checking in on him. I owe you lunch next time you're free!

For Hospitality

When friends or family open their home, or even just invite you over for dinner, saying thanks is a great way to show your appreciation. Include what was done for you and what you enjoyed about the experience.

Thank you so much for letting me stay at your place when I was visiting Seattle. It was awesome having you as a guide. I never knew there were so many specialty pet shops! Maybe I'll finally take your advice and get a cockatiel. Please let me know the next time you're in town so I can repay your kindness!

HOW TO LISTEN

Whether you're supporting a friend or just hearing someone talk about their day, listening is an important part of any social interaction. And it can be more complicated than it sounds, since conflict can happen when people don't feel heard. Follow these tips to help with active listening.

Use Nonverbal Cues

In face-to-face conversations, nonverbal cues, like leaning slightly forward and tilting your head, can help show that you're listening. The other person may also use facial expressions, tone, and gestures to signal how they feel.

Don't Interrupt

Try to give people time to fully express themselves. Pausing can allow someone to reflect on what they've just said and consider what they want to say next. Wait until they ask for your input before you jump in.

Avoid Judgment

It can be easy to jump to conclusions, especially when you're talking about something fraught. But sometimes it takes people time to fully explain the situation and get their feelings out. Try to withhold any judgment or criticism until you have a clear sense of what happened.

Ask Questions

Asking questions can help you better understand the situation, and it gives the other person space to explore what they're feeling. You can also use this time to clear up anything you think might be confusing or misunderstood.

Solutions vs. Validation

Sometimes, it's difficult to tell whether someone wants a solution to their problem, or just wants to be validated. It's always okay to ask, "Would you like suggestions, or would you prefer to vent?" And it may help to offer a hug.

HOW TO ARGUE

Sometimes conflict happens, even in the best relationships. When something is bothering you, bottling it up can make the situation worse than just getting it out in the open. But blowing up doesn't help, either. It's tricky, but there are healthy ways to discuss hurt and navigate conflict. If there's a conversation you've been putting off, follow these tips to get through it.

Argue with Respect

It can be difficult to communicate kindly when you're emotional, but some things are over the line. If you say something hurtful, apologize for it and take a step back. Showing respect for the person you're arguing with will prevent things from getting more heated.

Keep an Open Mind

Whoever you're fighting with may not have intended to hurt you. That doesn't make it okay, but it does mean you can be on the same team. Instead of you against them, it can be the two of you against the problem.

Similarly, when someone comes to you feeling hurt by your behavior, try to remember that you don't want to cause them pain either. You're not a bad person for making mistakes, so try not to make it about you as a person. Just give them space to get their feelings out, take some time to think if you need to, and then you can focus on solutions.

Share Your Feelings

Talk about your personal experience instead of flinging blame around, using statements that start with "I feel," "I want," or "I need." Starting with "you always…" or "you never…" puts focus on the other person's character instead of their actions, which could make them feel defensive and doesn't help them understand what you need.

Practice Active Listening

Listen to the person you're arguing with instead of focusing on how you're going to respond. Ask questions, and don't be afraid to slow down the conversation if it's getting confusing and hard.

Take a Break

If things are getting too heated, it's okay to take a break! Stepping back from an argument doesn't mean you're not invested in fixing the problem. It just means you want to come back to it when you're in the right headspace.

HOW TO APOLOGIZE

Everyone makes mistakes, and that's okay. If you're really sorry, an apology goes a long way toward making it right. It can be hard to know how to start, so follow these steps when reaching out.

1. Say what you're sorry for. Try to be specific. For example, instead of just saying that you're sorry for speaking rudely, try to acknowledge the specific things that you said.

2. Say why what you did was wrong or hurtful.

3. Accept responsibility for your behavior. Don't blame your behavior on something or someone else.

4. Have a plan for moving forward. Explain how you're going to make sure you don't repeat this behavior.

5. Ask for forgiveness. The person you're apologizing to might not immediately forgive you, but if your apology is sincere and if the relationship is built on trust, you may find that your friendship can be made even stronger through this honesty and vulnerability.

6. If someone brought this to your attention, thank them for doing so.

Put It in Practice:

I owe you an apology for interrupting you in class today. It was rude of me, and I see now how it made you feel like I didn't value your opinion. I'm going to make sure I listen better moving forward. I hope you can forgive me. Thank you for letting me know it bothered you.

I'm sorry for being so late to dinner today. I know it was frustrating to miss our reservation, and I can see how it made you feel like I don't value your time. Moving forward, I'll try to keep better track of my time, and if I'm running late, I'll make sure to let you know right away. I hope you can forgive me.

HOW TO GIVE A COMPLIMENT

A kind and thoughtful compliment can make someone's day! Follow these tips to make the people in your life feel appreciated.

Be Sincere

Tell people what you genuinely like or admire about them. Compliments are only valuable if you mean what you're saying.

Pick A Point of Pride

Has your friend been working hard on something? Let them know you think it's awesome. It's great to validate a person's effort and dedication.

Achievements Over Looks

There's nothing wrong with a well-placed, sincere "I love your shoes" or "Wow, great haircut!" But many people don't enjoy having their appearance commented on, even if that comment is positive. Instead, it's better to focus on choices and achievements. Congratulate someone on winning a writing contest, or making a good point in class.

Don't Be Backhanded

Try not to be passive-aggressive. Don't attach qualifiers or make implications. Saying something like "Your sense of style is so good lately" can imply that someone's style was bad before, and saying something like "You're good at basketball, for a newbie" turns a compliment into an insult.

MONEY, MONEY, MONEY

Let's be real—working, budgeting, and tracking your credit score (yes, really) aren't the fun parts of adulting. But all the other ups and downs of grown-up independence—an apartment to clean, food to eat, dinner dates to go on, and your own video games to buy—are connected to money. Turn the page for help navigating some of the sucky realities of jobs and finance.

JOB HUNTING

Job searching is the opposite of fun, but unless you can count on inheriting a private island, you'll probably have to do it at some point. Luckily, you're awesome, so you'll find something to do in no time. It may not be easy, but with these tips, you can tackle it with confidence. (Note that if you're under eighteen, there may be laws limiting what kind of work you can do, so make sure to check the work laws in your area before you start applying.)

Consider What You Like

Do you like kids? Or working with animals? Are you really good at math or swimming or coding? Narrow your search by considering what you enjoy and how you like to get things done. When you find a job you're interested in, check the pay ranges online before applying, and factor in how many hours you'll be able to work per week. Prioritize jobs that play to your strengths, and don't apply for a job you know you'll hate.

Look Online

The internet is a great place to look for jobs, and new ones get posted every single day! Many sites even let you save keywords so that you're notified whenever certain jobs appear. If you have a dream career in mind, look for job boards and newsletters connected to that specific industry. You might be part of a smaller applicant pool that way.

Look Locally

You may have an easier time finding a job if you look locally. Walk around the mall and see if there are any help wanted signs, check your school and library for job listings, and talk to family friends, older students, or other contacts about which businesses are hiring. If there's a place you want to work, you can always go there and inquire. Even if a business isn't currently looking to hire, if they know that you're interested, they may reach out when they're seeking new employees.

Offer Your Services

You can get some jobs yourself with a bit of initiative. If you want to babysit, shovel snow, tutor, or do some landscaping, try creating flyers to advertise your skills. You can hang these in libraries, coffee shops, or even drop them off in mailboxes around your neighborhood. Plus, because you're working for yourself, you get to set the price.

Common Jobs for Teens

- Animal shelter volunteer
- Babysitter
- Camp counselor
- Cashier
- Pet sitter
- Dog walker
- Grocery bagger
- Movie theater usher

- Office assistant
- Restaurant host
- Retail clerk
- Snow shoveler
- Swim instructor
- Tutor
- Waiter
- Umpire

Some jobs benefit from a little training! Check the requirements to see if you need any certifications or experience to apply.

BUILDING A RÉSUMÉ

Don't worry, you can do it. (Yes, even if you've never had a job before.)

Contact Information

Include your name, location, email, and the best number to reach you. This way, an employer can contact you if they're interested in your application.

Education

List the name of your school and what year you're in. GPA is optional.

Work History

If you don't have previous job experience, you can include volunteer work, club involvement, and afterschool activities. List the experience in reverse chronological order, and describe the duties for each job in bullet points. If you're still involved in a club, use the present tense, and if you worked somewhere previously, use the past tense. Also list the time spent at each job.

Keep it brief—no more than one line for each bullet point, and no need for complete sentences. It's best to start each bullet point with a strong, active verb, like "Organize food donations," "Create flyers for animal adoptions," "Assisted with research," or "Operated checkout lanes."

Skills

Include a list of your relevant skills. Typically, employers are looking for hard skills (specific technical knowledge) as opposed to soft skills (interpersonal and time management abilities) in this section. Computer skills, second languages, and other practical abilities will help you stand out.

Formatting

Use a clear, simple design that's easy to read at a glance. Remember to proofread; typos and inconsistencies are a quick turnoff. It's easy to miss your own mistakes, so ask someone else to give it a second look for you.

NICOLE SMITH

Some Town, Anywhere / 123-456-7891 / nicolesmith@email.com

EDUCATION

Some Town High School / 3.7 GPA
Class of 2026

EXPERIENCE

Some Town School Newspaper, Editor
May 2022–Present
- Supervise the work of reporters
- Read copy to find and correct errors in spelling, punctuation, and syntax
- Develop content ideas for seasonal issues

Some Town Animal Shelter, Volunteer
September 2021–April 2022
- Maintained and cleaned boarding areas
- Socialized young animals to prepare them for adoption
- Advocated for responsible pet ownership through the shelter's social media

Some Town Swimming, Instructor
June 2021–August 2021
- Led structured practices for beginner swimming lessons
- Coordinated swim competitions

SKILLS

- Proficient in Spanish
- Microsoft Office, Adobe Acrobat, Instagram, WordPress

HONORS

- National Junior Honor Society 2024
- Editors to Watch Award 2025

CONTACT

12 Some Street
Some Town, State 12345

nicolesmith@email.com

123-456-7891

nicolesmithsomeone.com

CONQUERING THE COVER LETTER

Even more annoying than the résumé is the cover letter, and most jobs will ask that you send one in with your application. Cover letters let you expand on some of your experience to show why you'd be a great fit for the job. Luckily, once you've written your first cover letter, you can tailor it to fit future applications.

First Paragraph

Introduce yourself. How did you discover this job opportunity? Why do you want to work for this employer? What about this employer impresses you? Be specific—convince them you want *this* job, not just any job. If the position isn't really your dream job, it's okay to exaggerate your enthusiasm a little. You'll want to tweak this paragraph with every new application.

Body Paragraphs

Speak in more depth about your relevant skills. Read the job posting to find out what skills and qualities they're looking for, then use that language to explain why you're a perfect fit. You can also talk about the company culture and why you think you would add to it.

Feel free to brag here. If you worked a $300 cash register or your team collected fifty new food bank donations, that's impressive information to include.

Once you've written this section, you can easily make tweaks here and there to reuse it in future applications.

Last Paragraph

Finish your letter by reiterating your interest in the position, sharing your contact information, and thanking the hiring manager for their time. And don't forget to proofread!

Nicole Smith
12 Some Street
Some Town, State 12345

March 10th

Dear Mr. Franklin,

I am writing to express my interest in the summer internship at *A Real Magazine*. I learned about the opening through the student center at my school and have closely followed your publication for some time. I actually first read Jane Doe's poetry in last year's issue! I admire your magazine's commitment to seeking out emerging writers and creating beautiful print issues, and I believe that I would be a great fit for the internship.

I'm currently an editor for my high school newspaper, where I developed my skills as a proofreader through reviewing the work submitted by reporters on my team. Working as an editor has also given me the chance to practice laying out issues in black and white. I'd love the opportunity to help develop larger projects and organize print issues in color at *A Real Magazine*.

I believe that social media is key to connecting with a wider audience, and I think that I can help promote emerging writers by developing your online presence. At Some Town Animal Shelter, I used Instagram to connect with the larger animal-loving community and feature available pets, which resulted in a 10% increase in adoptions. I believe that I could help your social media campaign reach an even wider audience of readers by making use of post scheduling and infographics.

Thank you for your consideration. I look forward to hearing from you, at your earliest convenience, to discuss how my experience and qualifications may prove valuable to your publication. I've attached my résumé and a list of references. I can be reached at nicolesmith@email.com.

Sincerely,

Nicole Smith

HOW TO KICK BUTT AT AN INTERVIEW

If your résumé and cover letter go over well, you'll get to interview. This is your chance to prove you're an awesome candidate—and an opportunity to gauge whether this job is right for you, too! Interviews can be tricky, but with a bit of preparation, you'll be ready for any question that comes your way.

Know Your Skills

Your cover letter and résumé gave you a head start on this one. Review them and look over the job requirements again. Think of any skills and strengths you have that match the requirements, and keep them in mind when you walk through that door.

Research the Job

Look for info on this type of job, and read up on the company you're interviewing for. It'll score you points if you show you've at least looked at their website and can speak to some specific things they do. Having a good grasp of the job description will also prepare you for the questions you may be asked at the interview.

Practice, Practice, Practice

Find a friend or family member and practice for your interview! Common and specialized interview questions can be found online, and practicing your answers will help you get comfortable with talking about yourself. Remember: Don't downplay your achievements, talk them up!

Prepare Your Materials

Even though almost everything is digital now, it can be helpful to bring a paper copy of your résumé and cover letter to the interview. This will make it easier for you to reference them, and you can also give them to the hiring manager if they don't have your materials on hand.

Ask Questions

This is your best chance to learn about the work environment—not just whether you're a fit for the company, but whether it's a fit for you. The interviewer will probably ask if you have any questions at the end, and it's good to be prepared with one or two. Asking questions helps you come across as a thoughtful candidate who's truly interested in the job. Here are some examples:

- Can you describe a typical day for someone in this position?
- What do you hope someone will accomplish in their first few months in this position?
- How would you describe the workplace culture here?

Say Thank You

At the end of your interview, make sure to say thank you! Then, after your interview, send a quick email to thank them again for speaking with you. It's an easy way to be polite and make yourself a bit more memorable.

OPENING A BANK ACCOUNT

When you're pulling in big babysitting bucks or making midnight snack runs with your dormmates, storing money in a shoebox just won't cut it. Having your own bank account is a great step toward independence. You often need to be eighteen or older to open a personal account. If you're a minor, you can usually open a joint account with a parent or guardian.

Pick an Account

Decide what type of bank account you'd like to open.

A **checking account** is for everyday purchases. It comes with a checkbook and debit card, and you can easily use it to pay for what you need. It doesn't accrue interest, though.

A **savings account** will gain interest (slowly). The more money you save, the more that money will grow. You can withdraw money from a savings account, but a bit less easily, so it's a good buffer against random splurges.

Get Your Documents Together

Look online or call the bank to double-check what documents you need to open an account. You'll most likely need:

- Government ID (like a license or passport)
- Second form of ID (like a Social Security card, a bill with your name and address, or your birth certificate)
- Your Social Security number

Ask Questions

It's better to ask up front than get caught off guard by extra fees. The bank can help with questions like:

- Are there monthly service fees? Is there a minimum balance I need to avoid them?

- Are there fees for using ATMs?

- Do you offer low balance alerts?

- What online and mobile access do you offer?

- How do I avoid overdraft fees?

Have Some Cash

You need to have the minimum balance on hand before you open an account. Find out what that minimum is so that you can save up. If you want to learn more about saving and budgeting, check out page 116.

HOW TO WRITE A CHECK

It's easier than it looks. Just fill out each section as described!

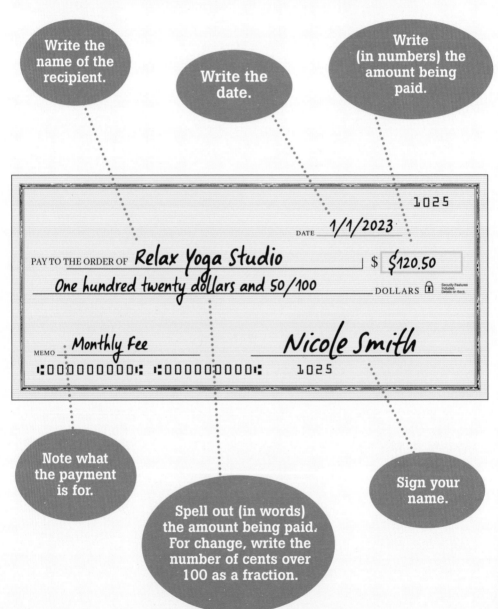

Write the name of the recipient.

Write the date.

Write (in numbers) the amount being paid.

DATE 1/1/2023

1025

PAY TO THE ORDER OF *Relax Yoga Studio* $ $120.50

One hundred twenty dollars and 50/100 ——— DOLLARS

Security Features Included. Details on Back.

MEMO *Monthly Fee* *Nicole Smith*

⑆000000000⑆ ⑆0000000000⑆ 1025

Note what the payment is for.

Spell out (in words) the amount being paid. For change, write the number of cents over 100 as a fraction.

Sign your name.

HOW TO SPOT A SCAM

Some scams are pretty obvious, like the million and one calls about your car's extended warranty, but other scams can catch you off guard. Use these warning signs to guide you.

Too Good to Be True

If only the texts and emails about huge sums of money or gift cards were legit. Unfortunately, if it sounds too good to be true, it probably is. And if it sounds too good to be true and you're being asked to provide sensitive information or money up front, it's definitely a scam.

Texts About Your Money

Your bank will rarely text you, and when they do, they'll also be sending you an email. If you get a lone text telling you that you've suddenly lost a lot of money, or that there's been "suspicious activity" on your account (along with a link to click), it's almost always a scam. If you're unsure, contact your bank using methods you can confirm, like the phone number on the back of your debit card, or your bank's official website/app.

Strange Spelling

If an email is filled with typos, is from a strange address, or has really wonky formatting, look into it before clicking any links or taking a requested action. Emails from your bank, school, or utility services will have formal language and decent formatting. All of these organizations should have contact information available, so if you're ever not sure, you can always call and ask.

Look-Alike Websites

Scammers can make websites that look pretty similar to the original. Check the URL. Do you see a .com that should be .org, .gov, or .edu? Is it based on a company's main URL (e.g. website.com/deals), or does it just use the company's name as part of a different address (e.g. website–deals.com)? When in doubt, you can also check the formatting and design quality.

TIPS FOR SAVING

Track Your Spending

Little things can add up fast, and tracking where your money goes may turn up some surprises. If you have online banking, it's pretty easy to track transactions and withdrawals. Once you have a grasp on your expenses and priorities, you can make adjustments if you need.

Do Some Meal Prep

It's no secret that eating out is more expensive than eating at home. But when you don't have meals planned, it can be hard to resist ordering in. When you add the cost of delivery to an already pricey meal, you've lost a big chunk of change. Instead of getting takeout, plan your meals in advance before you go grocery shopping. This can be a mix of easy meals (pasta with sauce, frozen pizza, etc.) and more involved recipes (pad thai, three-cheese lasagna, etc.) so that you'll always have something at home to eat regardless of your energy level. If you're looking for some easy recipes, check out page 42.

Shop Smart

Spending $20 four (or five!) times may feel more bearable than spending $100 once. But smaller, more frequent purchases instead of larger and more careful ones can often mean you end up spending more and getting less. Keep an eye out for deals and discounts, and stock up on your favorite stuff when you find it on sale. Check out reviews online before you buy anything big and important.

If you get the sudden urge to buy something you see online or in a storefront, wait it out and see if the need is still as strong in a few days or weeks. It'll help fend off buyer's remorse—plus, you'll always have an answer when someone asks what you'd like for your birthday or graduation.

Get Creative with Gifts

Have you ever heard that "it's the thought that counts?" Well, it's true. Expensive purchases don't automatically equal incredible gifts. If you spend time thinking about what your loved ones enjoy or need, you'll often find that you don't need to spend a ton of money to give them something they'll cherish. If you need help finding that perfect gift, check page 88.

GIVE YOURSELF SOME CREDIT

Even if you don't think you need one, getting a credit card early is a good idea. Building a credit score makes it way, way easier to get a loan or an apartment down the line. Just use your card carefully so you don't fall into debt.

You can get your first card at the bank you already have an account with. (For more on bank accounts, check page 106.) You'll probably have limited options at first, like a **secured card**, which requires a deposit for use, but you'll be eligible for more later if you use your card responsibly.

From there, building credit is simple. Just use your credit card to pay for things you'd already buy, like groceries and gas, then pay off those bills immediately. (You can make this even easier by setting up automatic payments with your bank.) You'll also have a **credit limit**, which is the total amount of money you can spend on your card before paying it off. Your credit score will go up as you prove to your bank that you can pay on time for everything you charge.

If you don't pay off everything you put on your card each month, you'll be charged **interest**, which is a sort of late fee from your bank. The more money

What makes up your credit score?

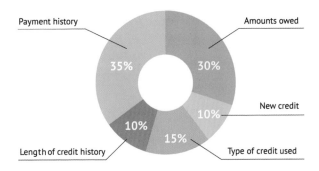

you owe, the more interest you'll be charged. Racking up interest charges can tank your credit score and put you into debt if you're not careful. Play it safe and stick to what you can afford.

One very quick way to build credit is for a parent or guardian to add you as an authorized user to their own credit card account. Using someone else's credit is a big responsibility, so you'll have to talk it over carefully before taking this step.

When shopping online, you may see offers that let you pay for purchases in interest-free installments. Unless you're making a necessary purchase that can't be postponed, it's best to avoid installment plans. The payments may seem small, but they can make budgeting trickier, especially if you pay for multiple things this way.

HOW TO READ A BANK STATEMENT

If you've opened a bank account, you probably get bank statements in the mail or online. It may look like gibberish, but it's worth understanding and checking out (at least from time to time).

A bank statement is a record of your account activity over about a month. They also go into detail regarding specific transactions, so they're helpful for monitoring your spending.

What Does It Mean?

Here's a quick guide to the terms on your bank statement!

- Starting balance – The money you started with.

- Ending balance – The money you ended with.

- Deposits – The money you put in yourself, plus any transfers from your employer, friends, family, and businesses.

- Withdrawals – The money taken out of your account.

- Interest – If you've earned interest on your account (which is likely if you have a savings account), you'll see the month's total here. The number will probably be low.

- Fees – Fees are not the same as withdrawals. This portion of the statement shows charges for overdrafts, returned checks, and ATM withdrawals. Check to make sure you're not behind on any payments.

- Daily balance detail – Use this to zoom in on your daily spending.

BANK STATEMENT

NAME	John Doe
ADDRESS	1234 Real Road
	Actual Place USA

ACCOUNT SUMMARY

STARTING BALANCE	1,221.55
DEPOSITS/ADDITIONS	2,400.00
ATM AND DEBIT WITHDRAWALS	-1,618.34
INTEREST	0.74
CHECKS	-20.00
FEES	-3.00
ENDING BALANCE	1,980.95

DEPOSITS/ADDITIONS

Date	Description	Amount
October 15	Payroll	2,400.00

ATM AND DEBIT SUBTRACTIONS

Date	Description	Amount
October 10	Car Payment	-425.00
October 19	Rent	-1,000.00
October 7	Debit Card Purchase - Restaurant	-90.34
October 15	Foreign ATM FEE	-3.00
October 15	ATM Withdrawal	-100

Withdrawals

Deposits

Balance

NICE WORK!
On average, you spend $1,100.00 less than you deposit each month

BUDGETING FOR BEGINNERS

Now you're ready to go all in! Here's a relatively easy budget chart to track your income and spending. Don't worry about the sample subjects—you can change them to fit your life.

	Budget Amount	Actual Amount	Difference
INCOME			
Income (wages, allowance, etc.)			
Savings (planned or accrued in savings account)			
INCOME SUBTOTAL			
EXPENSES			
Bills			
Phone			
Car Payment			
Insurance			
Gas			
Groceries			
Fun			
Shopping			
Restaurants			
Entertainment			
EXPENSES SUBTOTAL			
NET INCOME (income minus expenses)			

WELCOME TO THE WORLD

There are a lot of skills that everyone knows are hard to master, and then there are the skills everyone just expects you to know already. Whether it's creating a work-life balance or just decoding some mind-boggling bureaucracy, we've got you covered.

HOW TO GET THINGS DONE

Terrible homework assignment? Huge test? Confusing project at work? Sometimes it can feel like there aren't enough hours in the day. Here are some tips to help you finish what you start (and still have time to actually enjoy yourself).

Use a To-Do List

Organizing your tasks and schedule for the day can give you a better sense of how you'll need to manage your time. Be specific when you make the list—if you set a task that's too vague, it will be hard to get started and hard to know when you're finished. If a task is too big, try breaking it down into smaller steps before you start. Turn the page for some sample types of to-do lists, and experiment to find what kind works best for you.

Organize Your Space

You're more productive (and calmer!) when your workspace is organized and stocked with the essentials. Clear the clutter off your desk so there's plenty of space for whatever you're working on. What you need to have on hand will change—sometimes you'll need a big stack of books or a million art supplies, and sometimes it'll just be you and your flash cards. Don't be afraid to change things up to fit the situation.

Balance Big and Little Tasks

Most days, you'll find that you have a mix of simple tasks (like sending an email) and complex tasks (like getting up the guts to send an email). Focusing on all your hardest tasks first can burn you out. Finishing your easy tasks first can make you dread the big tasks more. Try to order your tasks so that each time you complete something difficult, you can move on to something a little less painful. Feel free to change up your priorities to fit what you can handle on a given day! Everything you do counts—it's not all or nothing.

Remove Distractions

Checking your phone every five seconds just stretches out your getting-things-done time indefinitely. To really get the most out of your time, put your phone on Do Not Disturb, and try browser extensions and apps that temporarily block social media and other distracting sites.

Take Breaks

Working nonstop is bad for both your productivity and your mental health. Short breaks throughout the day and longer breaks throughout the week will help you recharge and keep you from getting overwhelmed. For more tips on this, check out page 124.

Avoid Multitasking

Even when you're feeling like a superhero, it isn't really possible to do two things at once. When you multitask, you're really just task-switching, moving back and forth between different assignments too quickly to truly focus on any of them. It's less efficient, and you're much likelier to make mistakes—so it actually ends up costing you time instead of saving it! Instead of dividing your attention, focus on one thing at a time.

THE ART OF THE TO-DO LIST

Option 1: The List

It's as straightforward as it sounds: Write down everything you have to do. If more tasks come up, add them to list. Cross out (or check off) each task when complete. It helps to have stuff on paper.

To Do:
☐ Write history paper
☐ Do dishes
☐ Make bed
☐ Call Angela
☐ Finish practice sheets
☐ Check on group project
☐ E-mail Mr. Smith
☐
☐
☐
☐
☐

Option 2: The Scheduler

Maybe you prefer to visualize when things will get done, rather than look at one big block of all the little things you need to do. Try something like this to split your day into bite-size pieces.

Morning	Midday	Evening
8 a.m. Wake up, get ready	12 p.m. Gym Class	7 p.m. Dinner
9 a.m. Biology—check out lab equipment	1 p.m. Lunch	8 p.m. Family Movie Night
10 a.m. English Lit	2 p.m. Free Period	10 p.m. Get ready for bed, sleep
11 a.m. Study Hall – review Calc notes	3 p.m Calculus – quiz!	
	4 p.m. Homework—Lit paper, Bio handouts	

Option 3: The Hierarchy of Tasks

If you know that a lot needs to get done but you're unsure how to start, break it down! Organize your tasks into high, medium, and low priority sections (or try the variation shown below). Every day, or a few times per week, move tasks to different sections as needed.

Today	Tomorrow	This Week
Calculus homework	Flash cards for Spanish test	Send out party invitations
Chapter 2 of history textbook	Take out trash	Call Grandma
Email math teacher about missing class	Macbeth essay outline	Beat Space Princess 3 on hard mode
Fold laundry	Soccer practice	Painting class
	Dinner with Sammy	
	Order new uniform	

Option 4: All of the Above (and More!)

A template for people who like everything in one place! Use the right side of the page for your schedule, and the left side for your tasks. Next to each task, write a number between 1 and 5, to rank its priority. Things rated 5 need to get done immediately, and things ranked 1 can be finished at a later date. There's even room for some general goals to keep in mind (or, if you'd prefer, a daily affirmation).

Tasks	
Finish self-assessment	4
Email English teacher	1
Study for math quiz	2
Pack for weekend trip	3

Goals	
Memorize quadratic formula	
Save money for trip	

Schedule	
8 a.m.	First classes start
9 a.m.	
10 a.m.	
11 a.m.	
12 p.m.	Lunch
1 p.m.	
2 p.m.	
3 p.m.	Classes End
4 p.m.	
5 p.m.	
6 p.m.	

HOW TO TAKE A BREAK

While it's true that on some days you'll have a lot to get through, that doesn't mean you should work nonstop. In fact, you should take frequent breaks throughout the day: 15- to 20-minute breaks for every 50 to 90 minutes of work. And hey! No task-switching allowed. Breaks are for relaxing, not doing other work.

Move Your Body

If you've been sitting still, it will feel great to get up and move around. Try:

- Walking around the block
- Dancing in your room
- Stretching

Limit Screen Time

It's hard to truly relax when you're just shifting your focus from one screen (your computer) to another (your phone). Instead, try:

- Listening to music
- Meditating (check out page 82)
- Writing or doodling

Fuel Your Brain

Your brain needs energy to work its best. Try:

- Eating a snack
- Getting a glass of water
- Drinking a smoothie (check out page 40)

Get Social

Spending time with others is a great way to relax and get your mind off work. Try:

- Walking with a coworker or classmate
- Calling someone on the phone
- Grabbing coffee or ice cream with a friend

Shift Your Attention

When you take a break, try using a different part of your brain. If you've been mostly reading or writing for work or study, you might not find yourself refreshed if you leaf through a magazine during your break. Even just changing location can reinvigorate your brain.

DEALING WITH HEALTH INSURANCE

Nobody wants to struggle with bureaucracy and paperwork, and it's especially hard when you're injured or sick. But if you live in the United States, most health care requires insurance. When you need medical help for any reason, you'll want to know what's covered, what isn't, and how to keep your brain from melting while you decode your plan and get the care you deserve.

If your parents have health insurance that covers you, you can stay on their plan until the end of the year you turn twenty-six (or the age permitted in your state). Otherwise, you can get insurance from some employers or from the U.S. government's **Health Insurance Marketplace**. You can get or change Marketplace plans during open enrollment periods or any time you have a **qualifying life event (QLE)**—moving, starting school, losing other health insurance, and more. You may be able to get free or low-cost care if you have a low income or other life factors. Find a health care navigator in your state to help walk you through it and find the right plan.*

Terms to Know

- **Deductible** – The amount you pay for health care services each year before your insurance begins to cover costs. Sometimes your plan will have separate deductibles for things like medication, or waive your deductible for certain covered services.

- **Coinsurance**** – A percentage of a covered health care service that you pay after you've met your deductible. If your plan has a 20 percent coinsurance, and a doctor's visit is $100, you would pay $20 for that visit and your insurance would cover the rest.

- **Copay**** – A fixed amount that you pay for covered health care services.

- **Out-of-pocket maximum** – The highest amount of money you'd have to spend for covered services each year. After spending this amount, your insurance will pay 100 percent for covered services the rest of the year. (Most people don't hit their out-of-pocket maximum unless they have very significant health care needs.)

- **Premium** – Monthly cost for health care coverage. Plans with lower premiums usually have higher deductibles, copayments and coinsurance, and out-of-pocket maximums. Plans with higher premiums typically offer lower deductibles, copayments and coinsurance, and out-of-pocket maximums.

- **Primary care physician** – Your main health care provider (often a doctor, physician assistant, or nurse practitioner) that you see for non-emergency situations.

- **Prior authorization** – A requirement that your provider gets approval from your health insurance before prescribing certain medications or performing certain procedures. Without this authorization, your insurance may not cover the treatment.

- **Referral requirement** – Certain plans require you to get a referral from your primary care doctor for specialized treatment before they will cover the cost. Check with your insurance before making an appointment.

*Health Insurance Marketplace information is specific to the United States and accurate at the time of this printing.

**Many plans have different copay and coinsurance requirements for different types of services. For example, you might pay $20 for your primary care physician, $50 to see a specialist, and 20 percent for an X-ray.

Insurance Card

You'll get a card from your insurance company that will help health care providers bill your insurance, charge you the correct amount, and keep you in their system. Here's a quick guide to reading yours.

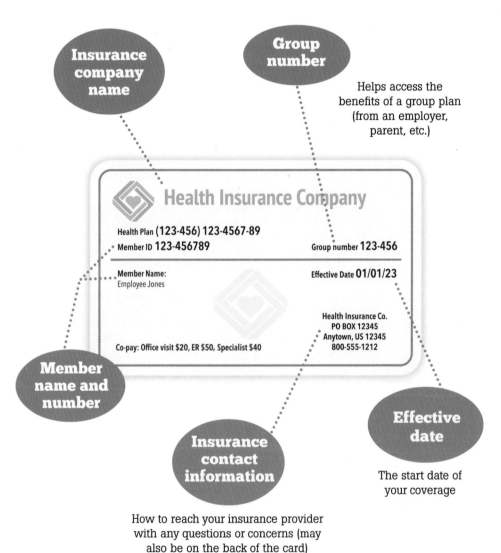

Insurance company name

Group number

Helps access the benefits of a group plan (from an employer, parent, etc.)

Health Plan (123-456) 123-4567-89
Member ID 123-456789

Group number 123-456

Member Name:
Employee Jones

Effective Date 01/01/23

Health Insurance Co.
PO BOX 12345
Anytown, US 12345
800-555-1212

Co-pay: Office visit $20, ER $50, Specialist $40

Health Insurance Company

Member name and number

Insurance contact information

How to reach your insurance provider with any questions or concerns (may also be on the back of the card)

Effective date

The start date of your coverage

EOBs, EXPLAINED

So after you get health care, your insurance provider will send an EOB, or Explanation of Benefits. It isn't a bill, but an explanation of charges.

our information and the claim umber for this service

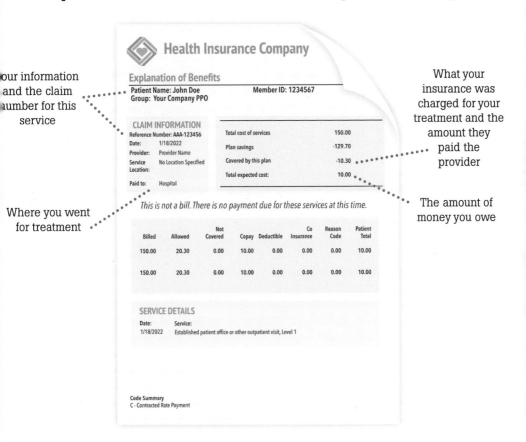

What your insurance was charged for your treatment and the amount they paid the provider

The amount of money you owe

Where you went for treatment

Health Insurance Company

Explanation of Benefits

Patient Name: John Doe   Member ID: 1234567
Group: Your Company PPO

CLAIM INFORMATION
Reference Number: AAA-123456
Date: 1/18/2022
Provider: Provider Name
Service   No Location Specified
Location:
Paid to: Hospital

Total cost of services	150.00
Plan savings	-129.70
Covered by this plan	-10.30
Total expected cost:	10.00

This is not a bill. There is no payment due for these services at this time.

Billed	Allowed	Not Covered	Copay	Deductible	Co Insurance	Reason Code	Patient Total
150.00	20.30	0.00	10.00	0.00	0.00	0.00	10.00
150.00	20.30	0.00	10.00	0.00	0.00	0.00	10.00

SERVICE DETAILS
Date: Service:
1/18/2022   Established patient office or other outpatient visit, Level 1

Code Summary
C - Contracted Rate Payment

Something not right?

Sometimes, your insurance or doctor's office can make billing errors and over-charge you. Check your EOB carefully to make sure you're only paying what you're supposed to. Use your claim number for reference when you call your insurance company to report the error! If you're denied coverage or receive a surprise bill, you can call your provider's billing office to negotiate your bill, discuss uninsured/underinsured discounts, and set up payment plans.

FINDING CREDIBLE INFORMATION

Whether you're writing a paper or just checking social media, you're flooded with information. But how can you tell if a source is credible or not? Here are a few first steps to finding the answer.

Authority

- Is the name of the author or group clearly displayed? Meme pages don't count.

- Can you find the author's credentials? Are they an expert on the topic, or just a random person?

- Is contact information for the author/publisher easily accessible?

Purpose

- Why was this work published?

- What's the bias? What point of view is the author trying to present? Does it line up with expectations you already have, or go against them?

- Is the source trying to sell you something? How obvious is that advertising?

Accuracy

- Does the work include sources for its claims and the facts it presents?

- Can you find the sources referenced in the work? Do any other sources back them up?

- Did the source go through some kind of review process before it was published or posted?

Relevance

- When was the source published?
- Has the website been updated recently?
- Is the source current enough for the issue you're researching?

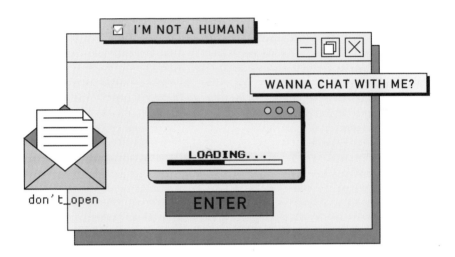

Watch out for this! *Sometimes, sources will confuse correlation (a relationship between two variables) and causation (one variable causing the other). For example, the revenue generated by arcades correlates with computer science degrees awarded in the U.S., but that doesn't mean arcades are inspiring more people to study computer science.*

ONLINE SAFETY BASICS

You've probably been on the internet forever, and you may or may not have been lectured about online privacy when you were growing up. A lot of information about the web goes out of date fast, but a few things are as true now as they've ever been. Some people out there don't mean well, and companies regularly mine your data and invade your privacy. If you don't protect yourself online, nobody will. Use these tips to get started.

Don't Share Sensitive Information

Be careful about the kind of information you share online. In the wrong hands, your address, phone number, birthday, Social Security number, or financial information could all be used to harm you, or to commit fraud by pretending to be you. Be careful about sharing your real full name or posting photos of yourself, too.

Check Your Settings

Strangers can access your posts and photos unless you specifically choose otherwise. The default settings on social media platforms often make your information public. Check your privacy settings to control who can see your posts. Try to limit how much of your info can be accessed and sold by companies, too.

Don't Click Weird Links

If you get an email or message with a link to click, it may be spam or spyware. Unfamiliar senders, long and sketchy URLs, and typos or weird robotic language are all red flags. You can also do a quick search of the message's text—usually, if it's a spam or phishing message, many people have already gotten it and posted about it online.

Check Your Passwords

Using the same password (or similar passwords) for many accounts may make it easier to remember your login info, but it also makes your data more vulnerable. Use complex passwords with a mix of upper and lowercase letters, numbers, and symbols. Don't use the same password for multiple accounts or share your password with others. If you think you may have had a data breach, or it's just been a while, change your passwords to be safe.

What About Wi-Fi?

You can find free Wi-Fi all over the place. But if a network isn't secured, it may not be safe. Be extra careful with your private information when you're on a public network.

Not Exactly Dangerous, But...

Some things won't get you hacked or put your information at risk, but you might not want to share them anyway. If there's information you only want your friends to know, you probably shouldn't post it to social media, even if your account is private. You never know who might share what without your permission, so if there's anything you'd like to keep private for sure, save it for real life instead.

DINING OUT

Late-night food runs are one of the best parts of adulting, and going out to eat with friends and family is a fun way to unwind and connect. Make the most of your meal with these guidelines.

Dining Etiquette Guide

- **Keep your phone off the table.** It's more polite to give your full attention to the people you're spending time with. If you need to make a phone call or send a quick text, that's fine, but excuse yourself before doing so.

- **Wait for everyone to be served before eating.** It's tempting to dig in right away, especially if you've been waiting for a bit and the food smells good, but it's kinder to wait until everyone has their meal in front of them. However, if the majority have been served, and you're given the okay, you can get started.

- **Treat the wait staff with respect.** You probably already know this, but it never goes without saying: The people who serve your meal deserve your respect. Treat them how you'd like to be treated at work. Say please and thank you, tip well, and remember, if something is wrong with the food, it isn't the waiter's fault.

- **Decide ahead of time how you'll split the bill.** This makes it easy to avoid any awkwardness when the bill comes, and allows you to let the waiter know ahead of time if you'd like separate checks.

Calculating the Tip

Generally, when going out to eat, you should tip at least 20 percent of your bill. If you get stressed doing math on the go, just try this trick:

1. Find how much you owe by looking at the bottom of the bill.

2. Move the decimal point one place to the left, and you have 10 percent. So for $20.00, 10 percent would be $2.00.

3. Double the number you just found, and there you go! That's your 20 percent tip.

If the service was great, feel free to tip more!

What about dinner at home?

If you're having a casual party with friends, you don't have to worry too much outside of making sure your home has enough food and places to sit. However, if you want to throw a dinner party (fancy!), use the guide below to impress your guests with the place settings.

DRESS CODES, DECODED

Obviously some parties are fancier than others. The real question is, fancy in what way? Your hippie cousin's wedding and a sorority event probably have different dress codes, whether or not they explicitly say so. Don't panic! Just use this guide to figure out a perfect outfit for your next event.

Casual

Casual dress codes are the least restrictive, but that doesn't mean you can wear your pajamas or clothes that belong in the wash. Take out your perfectly nice, fresh-smelling shirt, and you're basically good to go.

Events: low-key parties, local dinners

Wear: jeans, comfy shirts, sundresses

Avoid: flip-flops, stained clothing, shirts that stink

Business Casual

Business casual attire is perfect for the workplace and other professional events. If you have an office job, you may be expected to follow this code. You don't need to wear a full suit or tie, but you'll want to look a bit more polished than you might on a weekend.

Events: the office, business meetings, professional events

Wear: collared shirts, sweaters, dress pants, chinos, pencil skirts, blazers, professional closed-toe shoes

Avoid: sneakers, ripped jeans, wrinkled clothes

Semi-Formal

Semi-formal events are often held in the evening and require a bit of dressing up. Many weddings are semi-formal unless otherwise noted.

Events: fundraisers, weddings, engagement parties

Wear: casual suits, dress shirts, knee-length dresses and skirts, fancy jumpsuits, dress shoes

Avoid: boots, short dresses, tuxedos, oversized bags

Black Tie

Black tie dress codes are for important evening events like galas and lavish weddings. It's generally stricter than other dress codes, so don't be afraid to check in with a host or other guests about what to wear. Seriously, it's less embarrassing to send a quick text than to pack an extra outfit just in case.

Events: extravagant weddings, awards ceremonies, galas

Wear: tuxedos, evening dresses, dress shoes, formal jewelry, cufflinks

Avoid: standard suits, open-toe shoes, open-collar shirts

Okay, I think I messed up the outfit. What do I do?
While it's helpful to know the dress code of an event, it's important not to sweat it too much. If you've over- or under-dressed for the occasion, try to just enjoy yourself and be a gracious guest. A light joke about the attire can also cut some tension (either real or imagined).

HOW TO WRAP A GIFT IN 5 STEPS

Remember that perfect gift you put together on page 88, or that fancy nesting bowl set you got from the gift registry? Well, before you hand it over, you might want to wrap it. Here's what you do!

1. If your gift is weird-shaped, put it in a box before you start. Some easy (and free) boxes include shoeboxes or tissue boxes.

2. Cut a big piece of wrapping paper. It should be at least twice the length of your box. To check, lay the box on the paper and wrap it around the entire width of the box, then cut that amount off the roll.

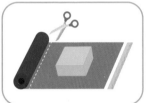

3. Wrap the paper around the box tightly and tape it along the seam. If it's much longer than the box, you can trim the extra.

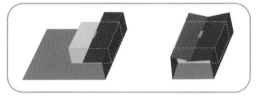

4. On each side of the box, tuck in the paper lengthwise and flatten, so that there are two triangles on the end.

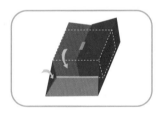

5. On each side, fold each triangle in and tape shut. And done! That's one crisp present.

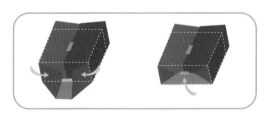

By the way

If you don't have much time (or energy), you can totally just put the gift in a nice bag with some tissue paper.

GOING PLACES

Whether it's going to the grocery store or traveling to new cities, how you choose to get around is a big part of Adulting 101. Granted, you might be going to the grocery store to stock up on limited edition Froot Loops and going to New York to visit the giant Lego store, but still! The best part of adulting is making your inner child's dreams come true.

BIKE SAFETY

Biking is efficient, environmentally friendly, and a great way to exercise. However, it comes with some risks. Protect yourself with these tips.

Wear a Helmet

Seriously, it's worth messing up your hair. Helmets have been shown to reduce the risk of serious head injury by nearly 70 percent. No matter how good you are at biking, there is always the chance of an accident, especially if you're traveling through busy or crowded areas. Wearing a helmet is one of the easiest ways to protect yourself.

Check Your Equipment

Before going for a ride, make sure your bike is in top condition to ensure maximum safety. If you're unsure what to look for, check the following:

- Are the tires inflated?
- Is the chain properly set up?
- Are the reflectors working?

Limit Distractions

Don't look at your phone, and keep your eyes on the road. Focusing on your surroundings can protect you from accidents and injury. If you need to drink, make sure to use a bottle that can be easily opened and closed with one hand.

Wear Reflective Materials

In the dark, you want to make sure that other people, especially drivers, can see you. Wearing reflective clothing will help you stand out in the absence of natural light.

Stay off the Sidewalk

Cars are a danger to you, but as a bicyclist, you are a danger to pedestrians. On the sidewalk, you could crash into another person. Sidewalks are also more likely to be crowded, have objects like trees and tables in the way, and feature cracks and bumps that could cause you to lose balance. Instead, stick to bike lanes, which are parts of the road dedicated to cyclists.

Use Signals

Cars come with signals, and so do you! Use hand signals to communicate with other drivers and cyclists.

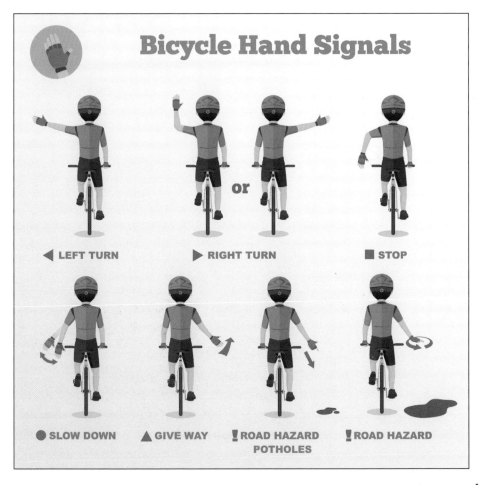

Bicycle Hand Signals

◀ LEFT TURN ▶ RIGHT TURN ■ STOP

● SLOW DOWN ▲ GIVE WAY ❗ROAD HAZARD POTHOLES ❗ROAD HAZARD

TAKING THE BUS

Public transport rules. You can take a nap and then be somewhere else when you wake up. Taking the bus requires a few fairly easy steps.

Finding Your Bus

1. Look up your route. You can find this information on a physical map or online.

2. Check arrival and departure times to find out when you should arrive at your stop. Use travel apps and official transit sites to check for possible delays.

3. Check how much the fare costs and get a bus pass or exact change.

4. Get to your bus a little early. Traffic (or lack of it) can lead to slight schedule changes. Being early can prevent you from missing your ride.

5. Make sure you're getting on the right bus! The final destination, route number, or bus name will be displayed on the front or side of the bus.

Riding the Bus

1. Enter the bus at the front door and pay the fare, using your bus pass or exact change.

2. Respect your fellow travelers. Find an open seat and sit in it. If there are none, stand and hang on to a handle for balance, but try not to take up more space than you need. You can read more about bus etiquette on the next page.

3. Pull the signal cords by the windows as you approach your stop to alert the driver you'd like to get off. Often, a bus won't stop if no passengers are getting off or on.

4. Exit through the back door. This makes it easier for other passengers to get on the bus without having to wait for you.

What About the Subway?

Taking the subway is very similar to the bus. You still look up your route and departure times, and it helps to arrive a little early. However, you'll typically pay your fare before going underground (or reaching your platform), and the train will make every stop, so you don't have to be on quite as high alert.

HOW NOT TO BE THAT GUY ON PUBLIC TRANSIT

If you got report cards that called you "a pleasure to have in class," this one's for you. Treating your fellow passengers with respect is crucial for riding the bus, train, and subway.

Keep It Down

Music, audiobooks, or podcasts are a great way to unwind and pass the time on a long ride. Just make sure to use headphones instead of your phone speakers. Similarly, you might annoy other passengers if you have long, loud phone calls. If you absolutely have to use your phone, keep it short and quiet.

Offer Your Seat

Trains and buses have seats dedicated to pregnant, elderly, and disabled passengers. If you don't need these seats, sit somewhere else or stand. If those seats are all taken, it's kind to offer your seat to someone who needs it. However, don't deprive yourself of a seat if you need one as well! And don't judge others who are sitting—not everyone who needs a seat might "look" disabled.

Consider Space

You are not the main character of public transit, so only take one seat (unless your body itself takes up more space). Don't sprawl or put your bag on the seat next to you. If you're standing, hold your bag or backpack close to make more room for other passengers. Doing this also makes it easier for people to move past you as they get onboard and depart the vehicle.

Cover Your Nose and Mouth

If you have to sneeze or cough, do so into your elbow. If you're feeling sick, wear a mask to avoid spreading germs to other passengers.

Don't Be Rude About Food

It's best not to eat or drink on public transit if you can avoid it. It could bother other passengers (consider: allergies and stinky cheese), and if you make a mess, someone will have to clean it up. Plan to eat before or after the ride if you can.

Listen to Announcements

Sometimes those crackly speakers say something worth listening to. Announcements can alert you to route changes, delays, added stops, and ride policies. They may also tell you if your train car won't open at your destination, which will give you time to gather your stuff and move before you take a surprise trip to the next station.

HOW TO CHANGE A TIRE

What You Need

- **Jack** – Lifts your car off the ground
- **Wrench** – For your lug nuts
- **Spare tire** – A cheap, temporary tire to save the day if you get a flat. You can typically drive on one for about 50 miles (80 km).

What to Do

1. Find a safe place to pull over, turn on your hazard lights, and use your emergency brake.

2. Take out your jack, wrench, and spare tire.

3. Loosen the lug nuts with your wrench by turning them counterclockwise. Don't pull them off entirely.

4. Put the jack under the metal part of your car and use it to raise the tire off the ground.

5. Now remove the lug nuts and keep them in a safe spot.

6. Pull the tire directly toward your body to remove it.

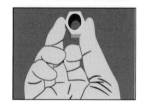

7. Place your spare tire on the wheelbase, lining up the holes with the lug nut posts. Push the spare onto the wheelbase.

8. Put the lug nuts on the spare tire, but don't tighten them all the way.

9. Use your jack to slowly lower your car until the spare tire begins to touch the ground. Then tighten the lug nuts in increments, alternating every other nut. This will keep your tire on straight.

10. Use your jack to lower your car completely. Then continue tightening your lug nuts in the same order until they can't get any tighter. Wow! That wasn't so bad. You looked cool.

11. Check the tire pressure on the spare, and take your flat tire to a technician.

Things you might want on hand:

- **Flashlight** – Helps if you're working in the dark

- **Gloves** – Protect your hands from injury

- **Rain poncho** – Helps if you're working in the rain

- **Tire gauge** – Measures your tire pressure

WHAT TO KEEP IN YOUR CAR

You probably don't need everything that's in your car—old water bottles, crumpled receipts, and stray french fries aren't exactly necessary for a smooth drive—but certain items can be extremely helpful in a pinch. Take a look at the list below to make sure that you have everything you need.

Handy List

- Tire pressure gauge – Measure your tire pressure! Impress your friends (just kidding).

- Jumper cables – When your car won't start, get it moving again with the help of just one friendly person (or one huge battery).

- Blanket – If your car gets stuck and it's cold out, you'll be glad you kept a blanket in your trunk.

- Flashlight/emergency light – Because sometimes the sun just isn't out. Good thing you've got this!

- Spare tire – Remember the previous page? This is for that.

- Hammer or window breaker – For serious emergencies only. If you can't open the car door, use this to break through the window.

- Socket wrench – Use this to loosen the lug nuts on your tires.

- Non-perishable snacks and a water bottle – If your car runs out of gas, you'll need strength to a) walk to the gas station or b) call your mom. A granola bar will do.

- First aid kit – Cuts and scrapes can happen anywhere. Truly, this book is a beacon of wisdom.

- Ice scraper – You can skip this if you live in a warm climate. If not, you will suffer without it.

- Portable charger – For your phone. (You know, the only thing more important than your life.)

- Tire jack – Lifts your car off the ground so you can change your tire.
- Windshield wiper fluid – Dead bugs and bird poop are no match for this. You can also get some at the gas station.
- Paper towels – Perfect for cleaning spills. Who knew?
- Owner's manual – Useful in any panic-inducing situation.
- License and registration – What can I say? It's the law, kid.

HOW TO CHECK YOUR OIL

If you like metaphors, consider this: Gas is the food that gives your car energy to get you where you need to go, and oil is the lifeblood that keeps it going. If you don't like metaphors, well, oil is still important.

Before you start, grab:

- Paper towels or a rag
- Your car's manual

Let's Get Started

1. Turn off your engine and put your car in park. Then, pop the hood. If you're not sure how, consult your owner's manual.

2. Find the dipstick. Look for a small, colored handle (usually yellow or orange and marked with an oilcan symbol).

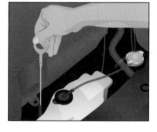

3. Pull out the dipstick by the handle and wipe any oil off its end. Then, insert it back into the tube.

4. Pull out the dipstick again and look at both sides to see where the oil is. All dipsticks have different ways of indicating the right oil level. Check for the letters L and H, the words MIN and MAX, or an area of crosshatching.

5. If the top of the oil is between the two marks or within the crosshatched area, the level is fine. If the oil is below the minimum mark or line, time to go get an oil change!

Anything else to look out for?

Yes! Check the oil's color. If it's brown or black, that's great! If it looks light and milky, it might mean coolant is leaking into the agent. Take your car to a mechanic, stat!

What type of oil is best?

Whether you plan on changing your oil yourself or going to a mechanic, there are three types of oil you can choose from: conventional, synthetic, and semi-synthetic. Conventional oil is the most affordable, but doesn't last very long. Synthetic oil is artificially created with additives that allow it to better protect and lubricate a car's engine. Semi-synthetic is a blend of the two, and is less expensive than synthetic oil while still offering some of the same benefits. Any of these three are good choices—it just depends on your preference.

Routine maintenance will help your car run safely and smoothly!

TRIP PLANNING, A TO Z

Determine Your Budget

Before you start planning your trip, figure out how much money you have to spend, as traveling can quickly rack up expenses. Check your budget (page 116, anyone?) and see how much you have saved. You can also research the costs of different locations and accommodations, which will help you determine where you'll go and how long you'll be there.

Pick a Location

It's not just about what you can afford, but also what you enjoy. Ask yourself some of these questions to narrow it down:

- Do I prefer warm or cold weather?
- Do I want to be in a big city or somewhere more remote?
- Do I want to relax or do lots of activities?
- Will I go alone or with other people?

Book Travel and Accommodation

Once you've figured out your budget and where you'd like to go, you need to start booking. Do this as far in advance as you can, as prices will go up the closer you cut it. You can also figure out what kinds of accommodations you'd like. You can:

- Stay in a hotel
- Rent a room or apartment
- Couch surf with a friend or family member

Plan Things to Do

To make the most of your trip, plan activities in advance. The last thing you want is to arrive at your destination and suddenly realize you're bored. Ask these questions to start:

- Are there any museums or attractions I'd like to visit?
- Do I want to explore any natural scenery?
- What restaurants do I want to try?
- When should I plan to rest?

Pack Accordingly

Now that you know where you're going and what you're doing, it's time to pack for your trip. Make sure to pack for your destination's climate and activities, and turn the page for packing tips!

HOW TO PACK FOR A TRIP

Before you take out your biggest suitcase, consider: Big suitcases suck. They're heavy, you have to check them at the airport, and uh, did you hear heavy? Use these tips to pack everything you need into a single, reasonable bag. Make sure to check weight limits for luggage ahead of time before you begin packing.

Make a Checklist

A week or so before your trip, make a list of everything you need to bring. That way, as the days pass, you can add anything you might have forgotten. This will save you from any last-minute panic that could lead to over-packing. It'll also help you rest easier, as you'll have lowered the chances of forgetting something important.

Plan Outfits Ahead of Time

Pack for the weather and the types of activities you'll be doing. You probably won't need a ball gown on safari, so keep it practical. And try these other tips:

- Pack versatile items, like pants that go with everything and nice shirts that can be dressed up or down.

- Wear bulky stuff like coats or sweatshirts during car and plane travel so you don't have to try stuffing them into your suitcase. (Don't overdo it, though, or you'll overheat.)

- Pack clothes that match. You'll be able to create multiple outfits out of just a few pieces if they all look good together.

- **Don't** go light on socks and underwear. Pack as many pairs as you think you'll need, plus one.

Use Space Wisely

Imagine you're playing Tetris with your suitcase. The goal should be to fill every inch of space (while leaving room for souvenirs, of course!). Here are some tips:

- Put socks inside shoes.

- Roll up your clothes (this will also minimize wrinkles).

- Use packing cubes. The smaller bags will help keep things compact and compartmentalized.

Go Travel Size

You don't need to take up a ton of space with your toiletries!
Buy travel-size bottles of necessities and leave the rest at home.

People usually forget...

- Toothbrushes
- Pajamas
- Socks
- Razors
- Sunscreen
- Deodorant

HOW TO ACE THE AIRPORT

Don't worry, all that's between you and your flight is one giant pit of despair (and an overpriced pretzel stand). Here's how to breeze through the airport.

Bring Your Own Snacks

Airports are sort of like big shopping malls, which means all the stuff they sell you will be overpriced. Protect your wallet by packing your own snacks. If you've got a long flight (or multiple flights, you poor soul), check out page 10 for some energy-sustaining combos. If you want to pack water, make sure to bring an empty water bottle that you can take through security.

Check in Early

For many flights, you can check in online up to twenty-four hours before your scheduled departure. Checking in early can sometimes result in earlier boarding groups and better seat selection. Plus, it means you can skip the ultra-long check-in lines at the airport, giving you more time to get through security and relax at the gate with your snacks. When you check in, you can also check the airport security guidelines to make sure you're in compliance.

Wear Layers

Layering not only saves crucial space in your suitcase, it also can make your trip comfier. The airport, airplane, and your destination will probably all be different temperatures, so layers will help keep you from being too hot or too cold. If your sweater starts to feel too warm, save space in your backpack by wrapping it around your waist.

Dress Comfortably

Repeat after me: I do not have to be the most stylish person at the airport. The most important thing is that you're comfortable. Sweatpants and slip-on shoes are worth their weight in gold on an hours-long flight. Plus, do you really want to be in the security line unlacing the double-knots on your combat boots?

Bring a Charger

The worst thing that could happen (aside from your flight getting canceled) is your phone dying halfway through your flight. Save yourself from tears by bringing your own charger. Don't want to worry about finding an outlet? Get a portable charger with its own battery. It'll come in handy throughout your trip.

Make Your Luggage Stand Out

Snap your suitcase up quicker at the baggage carousel by marking it with a colorful tag or ribbon. While you're at it, write your name and address on a luggage tag so the airport can easily return it to you if it gets lost.

Keep Essentials on You

If you're going on a longer trip or any trip that requires you to check luggage, make sure to keep some essentials in your carry-on. A change of clothes, toiletries, and electronics are important to keep on your person. If your luggage is lost, you'll be glad to have at least some of what you need while exploring a new place.

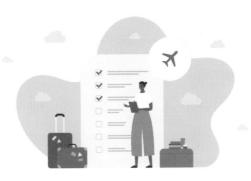

BE LIKE A TREE AND LEAF (FOR A HIKE!)

Yes, it is amazing to veg out on the couch watching old cartoons, but hikes in new places (and old!) are worth the heavy backpack and early start. If you haven't hiked before, here's how to plan your trip and decide what to bring.

Before Your Hike

- **Consider your skill level.** If you've never hiked before, find a trail that's suited for beginners. A challenge can be rewarding, but it's better to start slow and see how it feels than to go all in on your first trip.

- **Study your trail.** Mountains often have multiple trails that vary in difficulty and route, so you want to make sure that you're on the right one. Study the trail markers on your map so you can confidently travel.

- **Check the weather** and make sure you pack for what you need. Check out the essentials list so that you're never caught off guard.

- **Let people know where you're going,** just in case you get lost or hurt. Plus, if you tell someone you're going hiking, they might ask to join you!

Hiking Essentials

- **Good footwear** – Don't wear sandals up a mountain! Wear hiking boots with good traction, support, and protection.

- **Map and compass** – Because electronics are great, but not always reliable.

- **Water and purifier** – You need lots of water on any hike. A super-portable water purifier means you'll have enough to drink even if you run out! A good safety rule: Once you've drunk half of your water, turn around and head back.

- **Food** – Calorie-dense foods will give you the energy you need for your travels. Check out page 10 for snack-building tips!

- **First aid kit** – Having these tools is crucial if someone gets injured. Learn to use them in advance. You can find some tips on page 22.

- **Rain gear** – The weather app can (and will) lie to you. Dress in layers and bring gear that will protect you from the elements.

- **Safety items (light, fire, whistle)** – So you can start a fire, call for help, or see your map in an emergency.

- **Knife or multi-tool** – Handy for anything! Plus, it makes you look cool.

- **Sun protection** – Wear sunscreen even when it's overcast. Sun-protective clothing and hats are great, too.

- **Shelter** – A lightweight space blanket or emergency bivouac/bivvy is an easy, affordable way to shelter from the elements.

HOW TO FEEL AT HOME (WHEREVER YOU GO)

If you've made it this far, you're probably starting to think ahead to the future. Whether it's college or your first apartment, it can take time to feel truly comfortable in a new space. This discomfort won't last forever, but here are some tips to make it smoother.

Unpack Everything (Yes, Everything)

Living out of a suitcase and tripping over moving boxes sucks. Give yourself the joy of breaking down all that cardboard. Walking around your new space and seeing all your stuff there will make you feel more at home in no time.

Decorate

This is your space, so it's time to break out all the stuff that makes you you. Put those photos, lava lamps, and vintage posters on display! Decorating helps you make your living space reflect your interests and tastes. (If you're renting, check your lease to find out what you're allowed to do to the walls.)

Explore Your Neighborhood

Find your new favorite coffee shop, your new favorite deli, and your new favorite place to buy toilet paper. Learn how to get around without looking it up first. Find the nearest park and sit in it. You live here now! You and this new neighborhood should get to know each other.

Host a Party

Reasons to throw a housewarming party: good food, good company, and presents. Seriously, what could make a place feel more like home than celebrating with people you love? You can bond with neighbors, too!

And hey, thanks for reading!
Wherever you're headed, you've got this!